Published in German 2013,
Erleuchtung ist erreichbar. Praktische Schritte.
Editing Tina Ackermann
ISBN 3-9522513-2-4

Copyright@2013 Ruth Huber

English Print Edition 2017
Translation: Marianne Kuebler
Cover Photo: Jean-Louis van Durme
All rights reserved.

ISBN 978-3-9524816-0-8

www.ruth-huber.ch

ENLIGHTENMENT.
YOU CAN REACH IT.
PRACTICAL STEPS

RUTH HUBER

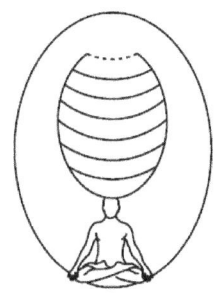

We all carry the spiritual potential within.
It hardly influences our life, or our awareness.
Until we decide to unfold it…

Content

Waking up, the First Step	13
Dear Friend	21
We Begin with Concentration in the Third Eye	24
Overview and Recap	28
Karma Yoga, Bhakti Yoga, Jnana Yoga	32
Chakras and Levels of Consciousness: The Basics	38
Charts	40
Relationship between Chakras and Spiritual Levels	42
Sleeping and Dreaming	45
Chakras: from Unoccupied to Enlightened	52
First Chakra – Root Chakra	57
Second Chakra – Hara	61
Third Chakra – Solar Plexus	68
Become the Hero of your Story!	75

A Useful Metaphor	76
Fourth Chakra – Heart	77
Fifth Chakra – Throat	84
Comparisons	88
The Sixth Chakra – our Third Eye	91
As You Can See, the Book Has not yet Come to an End.	96
Consistency and Logic	97
Development in Three Steps: Thesis – Antithesis – Synthesis	99
Energetic Communication	112
First Astral Region: Level 7	116
Stop! What Happened to the Crown Chakra?	127
Second Astral Region: Level 8	130
How to Recognize a Truthful Teacher?	139
Third Astral Region: Level 9	144
Cold-Hearted Psychopaths Rule the World	149

Let Us Taste the Sweetness of a Short Meditation	158
More on Level 9: "The Pact with the Devil"	161
Liberation of Beings	173
The Spiritual Realms	184
Compassion and All-Embracing Love on Level 10	192
Happiness and Joyful Creativity on Level 11	202
All Embracing Awareness on Level 12	208
Let's Summarize	213
Bliss on Level 13	218
Coming Home	220
The Numinous	222
It Is Time for the Ultimate Step	225
My First Conscious Dive	227
What now? What Is Different?	228
I Have already Mentioned It	230
God	231

My Spiritual Companions 238

Dear Reader, Dear Seeker, 244

Epilogue by Šárka Černochová 245

Ruth Huber 249

Waking up, the First Step

The word "esoteric" used to be the term to describe that inner knowledge that is not accessible to all and that leads to spirituality. The search for this true spirituality is like waking up. It is hundreds of years old and is present in many spiritual and philosophical traditions.

In the Sixties, a burst of consciousness manifested through the Hippie Movement in the USA. In those days, dogmatic codes of conduct were questioned and thrown overboard. The term "esoteric" promised a new access to knowledge, to spiritual awareness. This fantastic movement only lasted for a short while. "New Age" was turned into the new religion, in order to regain control on the burgeoning consciousness. Henry Kissinger is said to be the deviser of this "weapon".

Today, the term esoteric is often associated with "illusionary world view" and "naïve aestheticism".

Expectations and hope were in the air prior to the magical date December 21, 2012. A magnificent era was to come. The end of the Mayan Calendar allowed various interpretations. Shamans, astronomers, astrologers, archaeologists, remote-viewers, time-travellers, clairvoyants and all sorts of "channellers" gave their opinions and aired their views. And what has become of the predicted quantum-leap of consciousness levels on planet Earth?

There have certainly been changes. These are however so subtle that they remain unobserved by the majority, seen only by those who have worked for a long time towards a wide spiritual awareness or were born with such.

Fields of knowledge, so far completely separated from each other, are increasingly interconnected. This allows a clearer view on the history of the planet and the evolution of mankind. New insights on the nature of the universe mirror new definitions of the nature of consciousness. As within, so without! Moreover, it is widely acknowledged that telepathic contact is becoming easier. Making telepathic contact with the morphogenetic fields of knowledge will greatly accelerate your development.

Only a small part of humanity however can profit from these changes.

Shortly after year-end 2012/beginning of 2013 disenchantment set in. The expected overwhelming changes did not happen and people felt disillusioned.

This sobering is a chance. An opportunity to become free. Free of fixation on a date, a religion, an "Ersatz-religion", a dogma. Free for the path to true spirituality.

Whoever wants to reach higher consciousness, should dare to take a step ahead now! Freedom is not a gift. It requires determination, commitment and prudence.

The extensive influencing, conditioning and programming we are now submitted to, make it difficult for us to remain awake and in clarity.

We should realize that nowadays devices and programs exist that can project voices directly into the head of human beings. This "synthetic telepathy" is being used in shopping centres to deter clients from stealing, so it is said …

The same technology induced 8'000 Iraqi soldiers to spontaneously capitulate in March 2003, initially an unexplainable phenomenon. Later, the information was leaked.

Such examples shake us up. So do stories of so-called channellings of prophecies and teachings by angelic beings. Are the sources really so angelic? Could it be that the source actually is a secret power wanting to keep its flock of sheep under control?

We humans are being increasingly manipulated and we do not realize it. The heteronomy has reached such levels that the worst is to be feared. "Transhumanism", another example, is a method by which body and brain are enhanced by technical components ...

Such a machine-human is perfectly adapted to "the System". It will work without fatigue, without sick-leave. If it is well programmed, it will work reliably from the first day on, effortlessly integrating every upgrade until it needs to be recycled, without requiring any pension payments. It somehow reminds me of the colleagues at Sonmi 451 from "Cloud Atlas" by David Mitchell.

You may possibly be irritated by the examples I have given, all of them sounding like American conspiracy theories. I am not a fanatic and I am also not a doomsayer. Through intensive study of such phenomena, I have learned to see from the perspective of my Higher Self and to recognize the intention behind such events.

Moreover, there are many so-called "esoteric" (new age) beliefs circulating. I call them esoteric lies, but I could just as well call them nonsense or anaesthetic.

Examples of Esoteric Lies

- *All paths lead to the goal*
  How could they, when not all goals are the same?

- *All beings will eventually reach the final destination, some beings taking somewhat longer.*

  Which destination? Such statements are like sleeping pills... just as many other esoteric affirmations. They delay the awakening, they prevent the departure.

- *All beings will eventually be enlightened*

   How could that be, when they themselves do not even aim at such an enlightenment?
   It is an illusion! Whoever does not wake up during a lifetime, seeing himself as a being, instead of identifying himself solely with his body and his emotions, has no spiritual identity. Without the help of another being with freed consciousness, such a person will actually dissolve once it has become too weak to start a new incarnation: a speck of sadness goes in that direction, a quantum of lust goes in another direction, anger sticks to what makes angry.
   In order to free such a being, it is necessary to go back with him to the moment of his death. Only at that point, has the being the possibility of reorienting itself and the work of freeing the being can begin thereafter.

- *You will only be confronted with as much as you can handle*

   How then can those who break down, become ill, seek to forget by ingesting alcohol, those who kill themselves be explained?

- *We are here because we chose to be here.*
  Or: each one of us chooses his own parents.

   Such a choice would require consciousness and cognition. Only few of us have these capabilities. The ones who incarnate for the first time are generally too naïve. Those who have been here before are generally karmically bound, so that they do not have a choice. No free choice is possible for those who have distanced themselves from spiritual awareness and are entangled in selfish wishes.

- *At some point, we all said yes to what is happening*

   No, hardly! Considering the amount of suffering and injustice in this world, this is an unbelievably arrogant statement. As spiritual beings without a body we were at one time in a state of allowing: everything that happens may be just as it is. That does not mean that incarnated beings born in miserable surroundings have approved such a situation or even, as some esoterics believe, have themselves caused such squalid conditions.

Injustice and suffering are not to be glossed over. Wars, exploitation, famines and quite a few natural catastrophes have been initiated by people/beings having their own agenda.

- *It is all predetermined*

What sense would it make to go through a predetermined script? - It is all about learning to think autonomously, to differentiate and to take responsibility for our decisions.

- *Everything is already in us and we have to find our own answers*

It is correct that we carry the full spiritual potential in us. But as long as the potential is not awakened, it is simply a word with 9 characters and has no relevance whatsoever. We depend on someone to remind us of our potential, otherwise we will just turn around in circles.

- *There are no coincidences*

That is a matter of definition. Quite a few things arise and vanish in the logical consistency of an energetic game. But some things just synchronize. Sometimes it is a good match, sometimes a mismatch. However, events are not predetermined and tied together. There is no stage director as in the film "The Truman Show". And those who attempt to direct us in their show are not entitled to that role.

- *Everything is OK as it is*

From a spiritual point of view this statement is correct. As a human being, however, we should be capable of decidedly and powerfully utter a YES or a NO. Moreover, we need clear criteria to discern between salubrious or insalubrious, between ethical or unethical, significant or insignificant issues.

Freedom after 2012

So we have gone through 2012, "the end" of the Mayan calendar, without any dramatic changes. The expected ascension of the whole planet with its immense population – whoosh – into a higher dimension just did not happen. At the same time, many other nurtured illusions had to be given up.

The threat situation on our planet – and consequently to all of humankind and spiritual beings – persists. Unscrupulous greed, egotism, ruthlessness have led to exploitation, slavery, repression and pollution of our planet, to blatant injustice. They have dulled, blurred and obscured our spiritual consciousness. They have made us unfree and small.

It is time for clarity and objectivity.

It is time for real spirituality.

Real spirituality is dry, hardly enticing, utterly undramatic.

Real spirituality does not satisfy the needs of the ego. That is not intended nor expected.

Real spirituality raises us up to a greater overview, to truthfulness and to responsibility of a higher order.

Overview and responsibility lead to defying the destructive forces: not to be consumed by greed, not to fulfil our needs with consumerism and materialism, but to experience serenity and being.

Overview and responsibility lead to finding a way to live in this world, albeit seeing through the destructive game and offering conscious and silent resistance to defuse it. Day after day. For oneself. If possible, for others too.

This development, the step towards real spirituality, is in my view most urgent.

We can decide in favour of it – or not. But only a wholehearted decision in favour of a spiritual path will ensure the much needed spiritual support. A tepid decision will immediately invite the "opponents", who will stop all undecided ones from reaching deliverance with all available means.

Beware! Astral matters and spiritual matters are often confounded. The definition below should help to clarify:

Everything that can adequately raise us above the earthly and astral limitations and everything that frees the beings from the wheel of reincarnation and death can be described as spiritual.

Through appropriate spiritual practice we can awaken to what we really are: **immortal, inviolable spiritual beings with all-embracing consciousness.**

Our most important asset is our consciousness.

Perhaps not all steps described in this book are of importance to you. However, the descriptions will help you with a self-assessment. And they will give ideas for your introspective work. Find out where your weak points are and work on them. We will only be able to take with us, beyond death, what we have worked out. Work is needed most urgently where there is fear or anxiety!

Sometimes we feel our steps are too slow and too short. This is a sort of optical illusion that can be compared to a microfilm being projected enlarged on a screen. A very small inner change can bring fundamental transformation on the outside, giving us the feeling that we are in another universe.

Should you get stuck, loose courage or feel confused, write me an e-mail. You will find the contact information on my website www.ruth-huber.ch

I will do my best to help you overcome the obstacles.

Dear Friend

May I assist you and accompany you …?

In your spiritual quest, follow the logical practical steps in this book. The clear structure and sequence make it easy to find the themes on your way and they can inspire you on your path to reaching the highest degree of consciousness.

Everything I publish is based on my personal experience, gathered on my journey and during the many years of therapeutic work in my practice, as well as in the personal exchange with men and women I have met as clients and students, but also as friends.

Warning: This book is substantial. The contents could be enough for more than one lifetime! So do not overstrain yourself.

In order to avoid feelings of frustration and overload, I recommend not tackling too many subjects at the same time. Get yourself acquainted with the content and find out which subject is of interest to you at the moment. So you can use this book as a comprehensive reference.

It is my major concern to make the terms spirituality and enlightenment clear and comprehensible, in the broadest sense.

> *Each gracefully ecstatic moment,*
> *when everything feels absolutely perfect,*
> *when we feel self-contained,*
> *full of love and joy,*
> *when it seems we could peacefully permeate*
> *the whole universe,*
> *is a moment of enlightenment.*

Moments as described above come and go. It is my hope that all beings may experience such a moment.

These moments can be compared to the small bits offered in shops to tempt us: samples, teasers. An advance, so to say, on delight.

So, will you join me on the journey?

Many things will sound familiar, some will be new. This book should offer you guidance on your individual path.

The spiritual path was and is for me the most exciting and gratifying project of my life and its most important content during at least the last 35 years. The steps are logical and feasible. However, it is often difficult to describe them adequately with words.

With many years of teaching experience, I know how different people are. Some stumble where others just walk past ...

I hope that my broad spectrum of possible answers is helpful to many seekers.

Good to Know

There are smaller and bigger enlightenments.

Each chakra can be enlightened – or simply not.

Enlightenment is possible and is not at all an "act of mercy by an unknown god".

Enlightenment is not lasting. It can be forgotten. The fact that most human beings are in a state of dense, relative unconsciousness proves it. We were all enlightened at the beginning.

Let's go…

We Begin with Concentration in the Third Eye

Concentration in the Third Eye is an important aspect of my teaching. The Third Eye is the seat of consciousness. We experience here a "seeing" that is undisturbed by emotions. We can "see" into our body, in our daily surroundings or even in the spiritual spheres.

Being able to concentrate effortlessly in the Third Eye is helpful for meditation and for spiritual work. So let's start with an exercise.

The Third Eye is inside your head, more or less at the height of the top edge of your ears.

In case this is new to you, do the following:

> *Imagine an apple. The apple appears on your inner display screen or somewhere in front of you. You are now looking with your Third Eye. The pictures are mostly blurred, as though you were looking through fogged up glass. You will soon get accustomed to it ...*
>
> *The place from which the picture is projected is your Third Eye. Its position can vary slightly. The Third Eye belongs to the energetic body and is not physical, even though it is associated with the pituitary gland and/or pineal gland, both of them situated in the centre of the head.*

At the beginning, concentrating in the Third Eye can be very tiring. If that is the case, then do it for short sequences several times a day. For example, whenever you have to wait or every time you hear a sudden tone or sound. Find something that will always remind you to go back to the Third Eye.

Remain playful. Short sequences, several times a day is more effective than trying hard to bring silence to your mind.

Silence, stillness, is the result of all-encompassing spiritual work. Trying to reach this stage right at the beginning leads to frustration. It is preferable to be like a honeybee, collecting small quantities of sweet nectar here and there. Your nectar could be: *"I am a free, spiritual being"*.

Enjoy this nectar time and time again. Just one phrase, a quick flash of joy – love – gratitude …

This habit will become dear to you and after a while your Third Eye will be your preferred window through which you look at the world.

Each chakra is such a window. Depending on its emotional staining and its corresponding themes, each chakra will determine how you see the world. The most objective and clearest view, however, will be from your Third Eye.

Do not worry about concentrating too much on your head with these exercises. We will provide for balance later on.

> *Make it a habit to return to your Third Eye every time you find yourself immersed in worldly situations or in very emotional states, or when you are in danger of getting lost in attachments.*
>
> *Take a short and deep breath and create a small, concentrated focal point within your head.*
>
> *Repeat this once or twice, or more. Repeat it for as long as necessary until you feel concentration has stabilised.*
>
> *As soon as you feel tense, you relax again and observe (or visualize) for a while how the energy flows through your body, from top to bottom, and then into the ground.*

This exercise gives us the feeling of sitting quietly on the banks of the sacred River Ganges, just observing the flow of water and reminding us that we are free spiritual beings.

> *And just before we become that flow (and merge with it), we concentrate again on a small dot not larger than a pea.*

If it is helpful, you can also visualize the picture of a small flame in your Third Eye.

With this exercise we strengthen a "muscle" that is extremely important for all sorts of spiritual work.

At the beginning it will be concentration alternating with relaxation. One minute of each is enough, there and back ...

With more experience, you will find out that concentration and relaxation are both possible at the same time: a very natural relaxed focus, without any stress.

After 2 to 5 minutes you allow your breath to return to its own rhythm.
That feels good, like coming home, oh what a joy ...!
Make yourself comfortable in this inner room.

Sometimes it feels like a cave – and you sit there very calmly, like a golden Buddha ...

Sometimes it feels like the top of a mountain, endless space around you...

Sometimes you feel like being in the top room of a lighthouse...

Always come back to this place with a deep breath (inhale). Then exhale while keeping the concentration and observe how the cleansing energy flows through your body, from top to bottom, into the ground.

Short sequences are efficient. Even 30 seconds are long enough. At the end of the day, you take some more time, making sure the energy flows unhindered. This has a healing effect on the body, cleansing it from top to bottom. Additionally, the emotions will subside and the mind will become clearer.

Create energetic openings in your hand palms and soles of your feet by deciding these openings are there. Don't worry, it will work! These secondary chakras already exist there, we are just strengthening them.

Repeating a mantra can be of great help, thereby attaching our mind to a chosen subject.

The old Indian mantra "I am" will take you to a subtle consciousness. You can repeat it softly and then linger on, being aware that you are.

Rhythmical repeating can easily put you in a trance. That is not helpful on the path to spiritual awakening. I therefore recommend changing your rhythm frequently or saying the word or sentence just once and then remaining in still concentration, staying in touch with it, feeling you are, not "saying" it.

Overview and Recap

There is no doubt: we all come from the divine Source. I call it the Numinous.

The Numinous is unity. No observer, no object. Therefore, there is nothing to say about the Numinous.

Whatever I might say about the Numinous is incorrect and correct at the same time.

The Numinous is nothing – it is all – but all potential.

The Numinous is eternal – yet timeless – permanent now.

The Numinous is everywhere – it cannot be located – it is beyond space and time.

Why then is the Numinous of interest?
The question is justified.

Knowing about the Source of it all and being anchored there, giving this allegiance absolute priority, will connect you with eternal being. After healing on all levels has taken place, the eternal perfect essence will flow from you – without ever drying up.

The goal of spiritual work is not to coalesce with the Numinous and to disappear for all times. Beings may wish to merge for a little while, to have a pause. I myself plunge in it while my body is at rest during the night. Free spiritual beings, however, prefer to remain present in whatever form they chose.

There is no other Source, not even for the "devil", "daemons", Reptilians or any ETs. Beings are beings. Alive or dead, good or bad. They are all divine, whether you like this idea or not.

Today there are also robots, androids, clones and programmes. Therefore, it can be important to find out: *"Am I in contact with a being or just with a cleverly disguised machine, a programme?"*

As a rule, it is still mostly beings we come in contact with. Some of them, however, have gone through such suffering, hardly anything human still remains in them.

Some of the beings have become destructive because they just were not successful with their constructive efforts. Others were traumatised, programmed, hypnotised, and some are trapped in a lifeform or in the astral planes.

You need to know that consciousness can be so incredibly dense that the values invert. Evil then becomes good, the goal is not to thrive but to destroy. Humans and animals are flayed and ill-treated, nature is contaminated, poisoned and destroyed.

We have all got our share of programmes (cultural, religious, social, gender) or have been conditioned to function as slaves, workers or soldiers without complaining. That is normal on this planet – the big challenge is therefore: *"How can a programmed being free itself from the programmes?"*

It is these programmes that separate us from our divinity, letting us forget enlightenment and even driving us mad.

Whoever decides to go for it, gains the possibility to heal and to shake off the programmes, because the divine spark is indestructible.

It can be difficult, perhaps even impossible in just one lifetime. But: Enlightenment is possible. You can reach it. However, conscious spiritual work demands intelligence, power and endurance from the programmed person as well as from the accompanying one.

We start our journey with the chakras, thereby reaching a solid basis, becoming clearer and surer with every step of the way. It is a long journey – there are universes to be hiked through. But it is not a skyscraper with many floors where we have to leave each floor behind us on the way up. The spiritual universes can be reached without going through the "hell" of the astral planes.

The quality of your consciousness, astral or spiritual, will determine where you are.

Those who have not yet forgotten everything, may find that much of this is implicit, each new insight reminding them of an inner knowing. Others will need much endurance to come closer to the goal. Do not let yourself be discouraged.

Chakras Are Bridges between Spirit and Body

All spiritual spheres and all astral planes are mirrored in condensed form in your personal chakras. Therefore, every one of your personal chakras has a subtle equivalent in the spiritual realm. More on that later.

When we, as spiritual beings, undertake an initial connection with a body, we start in the Third Eye. From here we incarnate ("carne" means flesh), i.e. we slip into the body of flesh.

If our consciousness is intact at the start, i.e. not yet devalued through previous experiences, then we use every single chakra. That is the ideal situation.

Chakras are organs of perception and at the same time tools. Having reached the specific capabilities of our chakras, gives us a broadband of behaviour possibilities to interact with our fellow humans and the environment. This spectrum includes tolerance, but also defining limits, love, but also anger. We learn to allow, but also to say no. This gives us versatility, strengthens us and lets us meet the challenges of life in an ever more sovereign way.

Generally though, the actual situation is far from ideal. Most often only two or three chakras are inhabited and used. To make matters worse, the chakras used are often hurt and in a bad condition.

That accounts for emotionally unbalanced persons, who feel pushed around by life, but also impaired in their possibilities, misunderstood, disoriented.

One of the most important aims of this book is to demonstrate how we can actually connect with our chakras and how we can heal them.

Yes, we ourselves do that. It is not the world's responsibility. And: the effort is in any case worthwhile because eternity is very long and we only have in our possession that which we developed ourselves.

To be incarnated in a body makes it much simpler to obtain information than being in the spiritual spheres. Here on Earth we have access to books, guides, teachers. There is the Internet with texts and lectures. That can confuse us or it can accelerate our spiritual journey.

In the disconcerting diversity of spiritual paths, we can describe three major directions. They are based on our three main levels of action: instinct, feeling, consciousness. They represent an overall classification.

The Indian terms for these main directions are: Karma Yoga, Bhakti Yoga and Jnana Yoga. The word Yoga means yoke. So Yoga means that we undergo a certain discipline to walk a path leading us to spiritual consciousness.

Nowadays, the term Yoga is often used in connection with wellbeing and a modern lifestyle. Yoga holds the prospect of attaining health, beauty, fitness, flexibility, harmony, power.

That is ok. It is important for me to emphasize though that nobody becomes spiritual by doing a headstand. Spirituality is reached when we focus on spirituality. Yoga-Asanas can be a wonderful complement.

To be very clear: I use the term Yoga in its original meaning. As yoke, the path to real spirituality and enlightenment.

Karma Yoga, Bhakti Yoga, Jnana Yoga

All three of these directions can lead us to a certain type of enlightenment. There are different enlightenment conditions.

Of course, it would be best to experience all three of them during our lifetime. The triad makes our development complete. Having access to enough information on other cultures and traditions, it is nowadays absolutely possible to take all three paths.

In earlier times, the seeker normally stayed within his or her own spiritual religious culture – monks in monasteries, yogis in their ashrams. Seldom could they compare and evaluate. This one-sidedness strengthened the tendency to reincarnate in the same tradition.

However, our consciousness only expands when dichotomy and diversity are confronted and integrated.

You have most probably already walked part of the path to enlightenment otherwise you would not be reading this book. But perhaps nobody has told you so far where you actually stand.

A clear determination of your position on the path to developing your consciousness can be of great help. Otherwise, you might be in danger of taking the mad world around you as a reference and, consequently, feeling lost, improper and strange.

Karma Yoga

Karma Yoga is the discipline of selfless service. Its code of practice is: be in the here and now. Do whatever you do with your best presence.

Karma Yoga brings the concentration in the Hara (2nd chakra), in the middle of your belly, below the navel, as in the Zen meditation of the Japanese tradition.

> You are aware of your breath. You are the observer. When thoughts enter your mind, you let them drift away like clouds, and you go back to your breath.

To practice Karma Yoga, it is not absolutely necessary to sit on a cushion.

We can practice Karma Yoga while doing all of our chores, by being fully aware, giving our activities the best possible quality, i.e. being as clear, pure, true, loving and careful as possible and enjoying what is.

This quality of consciousness can always be practiced: when playing a musical instrument, when cooking or cleaning, while walking or singing, while loving.

To make love, to have sex with someone you love, can be a nature given, wonderful preparation for the spiritual journey.

> Can you remember how it felt when your skin touched the skin of your beloved one for the very first time ...?

> Awareness at all times – your spirituality will profit from it.

Maybe you are right in the middle of your Karma Yoga without knowing it. Perhaps you are practicing daily.

The quality of your experience depends on your capability to concentrate on the moment while relaxing at the same time, to surrender to the moment, to love – or to the Highest Consciousness.

Perhaps your personal experience will become what was shown in the film "Avatar": plants communicating with each other through light. The soles of the Avatar's feet and the hooves of the animals touching the root system in the ground trigger hundreds of sparking signals, embracing the whole forest in the happening.

The same thing happens in your body with the cells. The body is a universe where everything is in contact with everything else.

Focus and relaxation – love and compassion – devotion to the highest quality of your own essence and that of your counterpart – focus – relax – enjoy.

By being aware, all of these experiences can be useful in your spiritual journey.

Don't worry: you do not need a partner for it, nor do you need to be touched. The fireworks of love are always ready to start, sometimes from the second chakra, sometimes from the heart, sometimes even more subtly. A permeable system is always open to any flow.

It is a divine quality – pure – eternal. Be with it – enjoy.

Karma Yoga and Zen Meditation

There is no doubt that Zen meditation is a good technique. You learn to sit still, to hold your concentration, you are in the here and now. And it will become easier and easier for you to remain in that centeredness while doing your work.

Be careful not to get stuck in rituals.

Rituals are at best tools and stepping stones. But they can easily become traps. People tend to use rituals as a reference point ... after a certain time these are only empty behaviour rules, forms without content.

In my opinion, many people practicing Zen meditation intensively sit much too heavily on their cushion to ever be able to get touched by the unbelievable lightness and love of spiritual essence.

Do not spend too many years or decades with Zen – there is so much more to be discovered.

Bhakti Yoga

Bhakti Yoga is the path of love and devotion. Bhakti Yoga brings the concentration in the heart (4th chakra).

According to the teachings of Karma Yoga, selflessness in centred awareness will help to overcome the tendencies of the ego. Practitioners of Bhakti Yoga see the divine aspect in every bit of creation and serve that aspect with love and devotion.

Perhaps you practice Bhakti with your children? In your garden? In nature? Playing a musical instrument? Not every meditation is just sitting quietly.

It is Bhakti when your heart opens to something much greater than what is in the foreground. It is difficult to describe the touching feelings with words. The feelings are deep and fulfilling, sometimes leaving us speechless.

When your heart is open, every tree seems to smile at you, every insect, every single cell in your body. In such moments you are completely aware that life is full of miracles and you look at them with the highest respect. You feel that everything surrounding you has awareness.

During the time we practice Bhakti, we find orientation by addressing ourselves to "someone": that may be Jesus, Krishna, a mystic, a teacher or a master of your choice.

Oh yes, such role models have always existed and still exist in all cultures, for all seekers. We are never left alone here on Earth.

Further ahead in the book, I will also go into the astral illusions and delusions that so often confuse the seekers.

It is up to us to look for a truthful teacher. We have to take the initiative if we want to learn from them.

Living teachers, or such that have not been dead for a long time, are in any case to be favoured. Photos, audio recordings and videos facilitate the telepathic contact. Ancient tales that have been handed down for centuries offer too much scope for fantasy and wishful thinking. You cannot imagine how many different "jesuses" are being worshipped ...

The direct feedback from a living teacher is the best.

Important: all teachers and masters spoke to audiences in their time and culture. So it is quite possible that their verbal teachings do not quite fit in our life or in our culture.

It is different when we meet them during meditation. If we are capable of turning towards them with an open heart, then the highest qualities will be made available to us. They are role models, so that we can awaken the dormant qualities in us. It is often easier to recognize what is already ours by looking at a mirror. Role model functions are therefore necessary and helpful.

During the Bhakti phase we are often moved to tears. Destinies of others touch us deeply and the evil things in life can hardly be endured – our heart bleeds. It is now important to learn to elevate our consciousness to an angel's point of view (level 10). We are still full of compassion at this level, but we have an all-encompassing understanding of the situation, enabling us to let it be.

In some Bhakti groups we meet people behaving like little children: naïve, their feet not touching the ground, far away from any sense of reality, unable to bring balance to their lives. For them it is high time to bring the concentration point to the Third Eye.

Jnana Yoga

Jnana Yoga is the path of knowledge. It is the path I teach. Jnana Yoga leads us to a deep understanding of all levels.

Jnana Yoga brings the concentration to the Third Eye, activating the pituitary gland (Hypophysis) and the pineal gland (Epiphysis).

The Third Eye is the seat of consciousness. It is an advantage to hold the focus more and more here, giving us a free spiritual "sight":

- into the physical body
- into the world and the reality around us
- into the astral universes
- into the spiritual spheres

Our Third Eye is at its strongest when the instinctive levels (1st, 2nd and 3rd chakras) and the emotional aspect (4th chakra) are integrated, meaning they are liberated.

The veils will lift slowly. We are all capable of seeing, knowing, being aware and understanding because that is our true nature.

Spiritual knowledge makes us strong and at the same time humble.

Chakras and Levels of Consciousness: The Basics

Our personal chakras (1 to 6) are condensed manifestations of the astral and spiritual qualities of consciousness.

The *physical* manifestations exist in linear time and are transient.

The *astral* reality exists in greater time units but is still connected in a certain manner to space and time.

The *spiritual* levels are eternal, beyond space and time. Moving about in time - forwards, backwards, sideways - is a given in the spiritual levels.

The majority of the dead have no access to the spiritual spheres, simply because they do not remember them and because, unfortunately, they did not bother about them during their lifetime. They remember activities, remember their possessions, their emotions, their relationships and their sensitivities. They do not remember spiritual qualities.

If there is a longing for pure love and peace, for example, the dead will temporarily reach the spiritual realms. But as long as karmic relationships and attachments exist, the dead will be pulled back into astral levels or earthly regions. They have no free will.

After leaving the body behind, the majority of the deceased will continue with their customary activities, getting involved in similar games as during their life on Earth.

We know that from our dreams. They can also be the continuation of our everyday stories, taking place in astral realms while we sleep. More on dreams further in the book.

Correspondence of Glands

The chakra system is the energetic blueprint level in the body.

The gland system is very closely related to the chakras. Only by diving deeper into the condensed matter of the body, do we reach organs, bones, muscles, blood, etc.

1st chakra: adrenal glands

2nd chakra: gonads

3rd chakra: pancreas

4th chakra: thymus gland

5th chakra: thyroid gland

6th chakra: pituitary gland and pineal gland

7th chakra: is, according to my own chart, located in the astral regions.

My own chart of the chakras and levels of consciousness (see below) has proven its worth in my therapeutic work and it is very helpful for orientation.

Charts

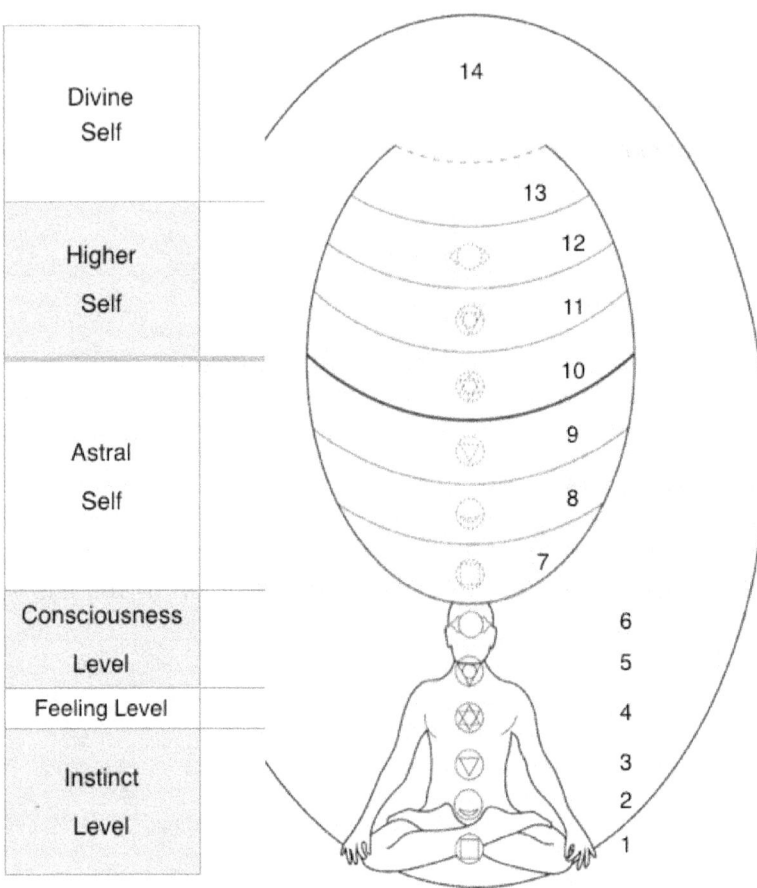

Divine Self	14	Unity, Source, the Numinous, Nameless
	13	Complete Focus on the Source
Higher Self	12	Comprehensive Perception
	11	Ideas of Playing
	10	Unconditional Love
Astral Self	9	Illusion of Highest Power and Glory
	8	Sexual Polarity, Astral Symbiosis
	7	Lowest Astral Illusional World, Delusional «Heaven», Dogmas, Programs
Consciousness Level	6	Seat of Consciousness, Portal to the Spiritual World
	5	Creativity, Communication, Clear Perception
Feeling Level	4	Compassion, Giving and Taking
Instinct Level	3	Emotional Insistence of Ego, Boundaries
	2	Longing for Symbiosis, Sexuality
	1	Survival

Relationship between Chakras and Spiritual Levels

The first three chakras (instinct) mirror the astral levels:

1st chakra – Level 7
2nd chakra – Level 8
3rd chakra – Level 9

The next three chakras 4, 5 and 6, are connected to the spiritual realms, i.e. to the Higher Self:

> 4th and 10th: personal love and unconditional love are closely related.
>
> 5th and 11th: joy of playing, sounds, colours, movement; are expressed in 5 with the body or with physical matter and in 11 they become a multidimensional ethereal happening.
>
> 6th and 12th: in the Third Eye we have the general sight over the physical existence, our surroundings;
> in 12 we have the overall picture of the complete spiritual realms, the universal happenings.

Levels 13 and 14 are beyond the Higher Self; they are the Highest Divine Self.

Retreating in deepest meditation, letting go of all earthly attachments and immersing yourself within, you may experience how it feels to be completely detached from everything animated.

And then, there are those "moments of grace" when we are overwhelmed by indescribable bliss. A nourishing and blissful immersion. At this precise moment, if we allow it, we might melt into the Numinous. The I will die - for a few seconds, for minutes or hours – the length of time is irrelevant.

Afterwards we are "reborn" knowing who we truly are and where we originally came from.

My Experience

I had the privilege of meeting Maharaj Charan Singh (1916 – 1990), an accomplished spiritual master in India.

Thousands of people had come to see the Master. As he came onto the stage, assisted by his helpers, it seemed that the helpers – although surely all pure souls - had more mass, more body surface than the Master himself. It's difficult to find the right words to describe my impression.

The Master however seemed to be the humblest person of all of us, at the same time radiating great personal dignity. This experience touched me deeply.

In our world, big egos are considered important and successful persons and they continuously stand in the limelight.

So we are used to recognizing ego power and charisma. Spirituality, however, is something completely different and can only be recognized by those who also have spiritual consciousness.

A really spiritual person is open and completely relaxed, straightforward and direct. There is no secretiveness, no mysterious allusions. Those expecting to see wonders will soon find this simplicity boring.

People who make use of astral powers will always be concerned about their fascinating image and surface (persona) shrouded in mystery. It is this effort that gives them mass. Through this secretiveness they enforce attention: *"I know something that you do not know (because I am very special) and I will tell you all about it one day, provided you are ready for it."*

This game leads to manipulation and dependence. Everything is very subtle at the beginning, hardly noticeable. A shining mask can hide so many lies.

Sleeping and Dreaming

As soon as we start with spiritual work, our quality of sleep will change, but not always for the best. It is therefore an advantage to know certain facts, in order to be able to influence matters.

Human beings do many different things while they sleep and dream. The question is whether the Third Eye is open or closed.

With a closed third eye

For 80% of the people, the focus during sleep falls to the level of the cells. In a way, we become like a vegetable. No point in feeling hurt – this happens to all of us from time to time.

During the R.E.M.-Phase (R.E.M. = rapid eye movement. During this phase blood pressure and pulse increase), our consciousness reaches a higher level and processes issues of our daily life. This is the original meaning of dreams: we are caught in self-made stories.

Dream readers with a psychological worldview offer the following opinion: *"Everything in your dream is you, whether it is a tree, a river, a house or other people. You are everything because the pictures come from within you. There is nobody else in this happening."*

This statement is both correct and incorrect at the same time.

In psychological therapy, where the objective is to reach information hidden deep in the subconscious, the dreamer is reoriented towards himself. There are definitely situations where this psychological procedure can be helpful. For quite a number of psychologists, nothing at all should come from the outside, everything is psyche, everything is within. At some point, this view becomes limiting.

For all involved in spiritual work the above procedure would be of little use because they have very real encounters with other beings during sleep or during meditation.

For those who are completely awake (realized souls), the situation is again different. They recognize everything as being part of themselves – but they are not dreaming, especially not emotionally loaded dreams.

When the third eye is open

As soon as the Third Eye is open, you will repeatedly immerse yourself in astral or spiritual universes while your body sleeps.

Everything spiritual has greater dimensions. We will only come into contact with it if the frequency of our consciousness is sufficiently subtle and if we welcome the contact. Spiritual beings are free and loving and have no intention to scare you, to hoax, to push, to pull, to trap or to shape you. They always wait for you to initiate contact and respect your free will. Sometimes we are surprised by a contact, because we have forgotten that we asked for it.

Spiritual qualities are a rewarding subject. More on that throughout the book.

It is especially the astral universes that come close to us during sleep, enveloping or invading us. Astral beings have intentions; emotions, problems and needs, and they often take the sleeping ones in their own "cinema". Many of them are stuck deep in horrible stories or traumatic happenings. They continuously scroll down these ugly pictures. Although these stories have nothing to do with us, we dream them, whether we like it or not.

Some astral beings have been ordered to confuse the dreamers, to scare them, to devaluate them or even to sexually abuse them.

The subjects and issues we are involved with during the day will determine the frequency of our consciousness. The dreaming theatre often tunes into the same frequency. It is therefore helpful to clear the emotions, to clean up the spiritual space and to lift our consciousness before going to sleep.

As already said above: For those who are completely awake (realized souls), they recognize everything as being part of themselves – but they are not dreaming, especially not emotionally loaded dreams.

The Dreaming Theatre Follows a Specific Programme

When the 1st chakra is hurt and has a lot of energy:

If you are anxious about your existence (work, house, food, money) or about your health, illness, death, you will often find yourself in one of the following dream cinemas:

Somebody is chasing you. You are standing on a cliff and you are on the verge of falling. A wild animal wants to chew you up. Someone has stolen all of your possessions. Your house is burning down. You lose your job. Someone threatens to kill you, etc.

When the 2nd chakra is hurt and needy and has a lot of energy:

The second chakra cinema is for all those who have great emotional longing for allegiance to a group or family and who have a deep need to be loved by all, or at least to be positively appreciated. A further important subject is sexuality and, connected herewith, a longing to be sought after and not to be dismissed, hurt, used, ignored, abused.

In the second chakra film you will be rejected by the group. You stand alone, nobody loves you. You are laughed at and humiliated.

As far as sexuality is concerned, everything can happen here. As long as you enjoy it, you would like to allow these dreams. I do not recommend it, because it becomes increasingly difficult to become free. Astral sexuality includes every sort of abuse. Once the door has been opened, it is difficult to shut it again.

When the 3rd chakra is hurt and has a lot of energy:

On this level we are fighters: sometimes we win, mostly however we lose. Suppose we are fighting against ten enemies and we win. The defeated will sooner or later also want to win. For this reason they will remain linked to us, so that they will be able to come into their own. If not in this life, then in the next one. That is how karma works. We do not get rid of our enemies so easily.

A Proposal – for Goodness (and for Relaxation)

Are you often busy in your life trying to prove how brilliant you are?

Are you providing your ego with a golden surface, which you polish on a daily basis?

That is very tiring.

If you have had enough of it, you can also stop doing it.

Only as spiritual beings are we perfect.

Wanting to be perfect as a human being is an illusion.

Ok, back to the subject.

Those who opt for challenging life from the third chakra will expand this fight even further in the dream theatre of the astral realms:

During sleep, the moral conduct code that normally acts as censorship during waking hours is switched off. In everyday life, we might have ourselves more or less under control. But during sleep the reins are loose. Emotions take control, unhindered by cultural and learned behaviour rules that normally define conduct in life.

And believe me: in the astral realms there are always enemies who are more powerful than you! Those who do not have a body fight with other weapons. Weapons you might not know of.

The real solution on the path to liberation is to engage in deep healing work with these three chakras.

As soon as these centres are enlightened, we will seldom only land in the astral realms, in these specific dream theatres.

> Sometimes during sleep, I also land in the astral spheres and I am then happy with myself when I act in accordance with the same ethical principles as I would here on Earth.

My Solution for the Moment

Do your mental hygiene before going to sleep:

> Close all open-end issues, end dialogues, find answers for questions that have kept you busy during the day. Write down which matters could not be brought to an end, so that they do not hinder you in your sleep.

> Find the love within you – or peacefulness, serenity. Relax.

> Obviously, the best would be to contact the spiritual, unconditional love. But that might not always be possible. It is good to know, however, that it is always within us, as our essence.

> By altering your frequency in such a manner, you will no longer be noticed in the astral realms.

> Give yourself a programme, such as: "I want to wake up as soon as I am dragged into an astral cinema!"

> After waking up you can give the astral film the ending you wish.

Do you remember what Morpheus said to Neo in the film "MATRIX"? "Some laws can be bent, others can be broken."

Practice while awake:

If the tiger was after you in your dream, go back to this situation after waking up. Now you spread your wings and fly away from the tiger.

If someone was following your steps in order to kill you, dream the sequence to an end while awake. You turn around, open your arms and say: "Try it! You will not be able to kill me because I am an immortal being!"

In the dream world you do not have a body to take care of. So nothing really can happen. Practice while awake until you act similarly in your dream.

Running behind the train in your dream? Not necessary! You just place yourself there where you want to be. We travel by thought.

Enjoy giving your dreams a creative and unusual ending.

This training is worth it. You will soon be able to "wake up" while dreaming and be capable of bending or breaking rules. This is called lucid dreaming.

As soon as you have mastered this, you will no longer land in astral cinemas. Once we have understood something, we become immune to it. Instead, you will now learn to spend your nights in the spiritual spheres.

Chakras:
from Unoccupied to Enlightened

Chakras can be in deep sleep, awake, inhabited or unoccupied. They can have too much or too little energy, they can be hurt or healed – or they can be enlightened. There is much to learn.

Maybe there are one or two, or even three of your chakras, you have not yet taken into your possession. If that is so, there is "no one at home" in these chakras. Your fellow human beings will consider you as inaccessible or boring on those levels and will soon avoid the corresponding themes in their relationship with you.

Chakras are tools we use with more or less skill. We are more talented in some areas than in others. However, we are on the winning side if we seriously try to improve or even surmount our weaknesses.

When a chakra, though inhabited, remains nearly empty, we feel somewhat needy and we have the urge to be fed by others as far as the theme of the chakra is concerned.

If a chakra has too much energy, we feel excessively energetic on the particular subject, perhaps even being overactive, driven or too expansive towards others.

Chakras can be relaxed or tensed up. Is a chakra relaxed, because we do not have any problems with the corresponding theme, then others will feel comfortable in our presence and in turn be themselves relaxed. For example, a relaxed, self-confident teacher will instil calmness amongst the students. If a particular subject causes tension, as a rule the energy will be blocked and we can no longer act freely. Correspondingly, the people we meet while being in such a situation will often be themselves inhibited.

Chakras are often hurt. Some of the chakra injuries are remnants of previous lives. Often, these injuries lie far away in the past and are no longer present in our memory. We normally shield ourselves from the pain by unconsciously wrapping a thick protective layer around us.

Chakras are sometimes occupied by foreign beings. Foreign occupants are spiritual beings, mostly deceased persons, who occupy chakras or attach themselves to the emotional or mental body. (Shamans invite foreign beings to occupy their chakras. These "helpers" are supposed to give special skills to the shaman and to increase his power. From a spiritual point of view, such foreign occupants are undesired because they contradict the principles of self-determination.) Very small beings also can occupy cells or attach themselves to the Body Intelligence, the software-program of the body. The Body Intelligence is a created entity that takes care of our health and is in charge of the survival of the body and the species.

Some foreign occupants remain quiet, at first. Sooner or later though, they will influence our emotions, our thoughts or our behaviour, depending on their needs and intentions. Or they irritate bodily functions and healing processes.

A short note on the emotional and the mental body might be helpful:

The emotional body permeates and surrounds the physical body. Its size varies between half an arm's and a full arm's length, when we are in good health. Fear, grief, insecurity or depression will decrease its size. Joy, enthusiasm, being in love increase its size. Foreign occupants can attach themselves to a certain frequency, amplifying the frequency or feeding on its energy.

The mental body is subtler, more flexible and larger. It contains societal, ideological or religious concepts, all sorts of dogmas, beliefs and programmes. Foreign occupants can attach themselves to these contents.

From a spiritual point of view, foreign occupants need to be liberated. They are not to be ostracized (exorcism), nor sent into the light (esotericism). I will go into the process of liberation later in the book.

Each of the chakras can be enlightened. These chakra enlightenments, or small enlightenments, come to be when the development process has successfully come to an end, when we are at rest, have no ego intentions, feel joyful and relaxed.

An unexperienced chakra may well emanate purity and light. The term "enlightened", however, is only applicable once painful experiences have been evaluated and healed. It is this inner healing process that enables us to rise above our own pain and that allows an understanding of the suffering of others.

To start, we have to know how it feels when we inhabit a chakra, when it has too much or too little energy, when it is hurting, blocked or occupied by something alien.

We are challenged to take a deep look at our life themes. All bruises need to be healed, just as all problems need to be addressed and not swept under the carpet, nor tagged with the excuse: *"That is me – I can't help it"; "As a child I was often left alone, beaten and abused"; "My father was an alcoholic, my mother depressive." Or: "My horoscopic sign is Taurus ..."*

As long as we utter such excuses and justifications, we are identifying ourselves with what happened.

Whatever experiences we have made and whatever programmes we have integrated, healing is possible from within - until both, experiences and programmes, do no longer matter.

A lot of truthful introspective work is necessary in order to become a mature, relaxed and happy person. Only once the process is completed, will we become aware of our inner treasure and our balance.

Emotional dependency is no longer an issue. As social beings, we remain in contact with others, but are at all times emotionally self-sufficient.

Therefore, an enlightened chakra is one that is experienced, has been healed and nourished; now resting in joyful serenity.

I am aware of the fact that spiritual work has gone out of fashion. It seems pretty outdated to seek enlightenment. It is uncool to have a teacher.

Unfortunately, it is a false conclusion to believe no effort is needed because we all carry perfection and enlightenment within ourselves.

Just put up a smile and declare to be enlightened?

That might work for those who never lost contact with their essence. But those beings cannot teach us because, not having incarnated as human beings, they have not gone through the journey. They have never experienced fear, devaluation, despair, agony. On planet Earth they are the unexperienced.

Even if the era of the great gurus has come to an end, we should still benefit from their spiritual experience and wisdom. There is no need to reinvent the wheel.

As already pointed out: potential is potential. As long as it has not been awakened, it has no impact whatsoever. Nothing appears by itself. The potential is there. Now, it should be manifested.

High time to start with practical work!!

It is wonderful to find out how to improve one's wellbeing by diagnosing one's own chakras and by improving their quality.

The time will come when your chakras will be enlightened – not permanently, however, but you will know how to alter them. It is like with window panes:

It is better to know how to clean windows rather than just having clean windows, because they will need cleaning again and again.

First Chakra – Root Chakra

The first chakra (root chakra) is located at the lower end of the spine.

Element: Earth, male quality.

It is an instinctive centre in charge of defending the body. Its themes are survival and securing existence.

This is the centre that allows us to fight or flight, depending on the danger.

The adrenal glands, which secrete Adrenaline, support this reflex. The brain will only be engaged later. Reasoning is not this chakra's task.

Whether a person opts for fighting or for flight depends, on the one hand, on the physical fitness (condition, age, etc.) and, on the other hand, also on the emotional, mental conditioning (upbringing, moral values, early experiences, etc.).

For some people a spider is reason enough to flee, others are enticed to fight at the sight of a crocodile.

During birth our first chakra is active. It is important that it is later able to relax. If it feels secure, it will do so -> see 2nd chakra.

Important: a lot of people enjoy the feeling of Adrenaline pulsating through their system. I am not going to discuss this here because meditation is better suited to a low level of Adrenaline.

The first chakra and its various conditions
- The chakra is not inhabited:
  The person is not really rooted, meaning the person has not really taken possession of this physical life. It feels as

though it would want to avoid getting wet feet. The person is not really prepared to get involved, frequently changing workplace and home address.

- The chakra is inhabited but has little energy:
  The person can be easily confused and is not confident to be able to handle earthly challenges.

- The chakra has too much energy:
  Currency seems to be the only acceptable measuring unit. There is a strong attachment to all material things, right up to a compulsive hoarding syndrome, because possessions suggest safety.

- The first chakra is enlightened:
  The person inhabits the whole body, right down to the small toe, and seems firmly rooted. There is this primordial trust in mother Earth who will feed it and support it. All difficulties can somehow be overcome. This confidence is there even though death is a natural part of the whole picture.

Fear is the emotion of the first chakra

Important: Greed is not the correct answer to fear.

Whenever greed was the driving force, the result was generally destruction. A significant part of the unbelievable suffering in the Third World is due to the greed of the people in the industrialized countries. They believe the world to be a self-service store, where one can buy as cheaply as possible, without taking any responsibility.

A simple and truthful lifestyle would be desirable. We ourselves determine the target value by asking ourselves: should it be multiplied, would our lifestyle lead to an improvement or to a degradation of the situation on Earth?

The first chakra can learn to feel secure once we realize:

- life in this incarnation is temporary

- and instead a spiritual existence is eternal

We have forgotten to include illness and death in our worldview. Thousands may die during an earthquake, a tsunami or in faraway wars, without this fact really touching us. Instead, we are overwhelmed when someone close unexpectedly falls ill, dies or commits suicide.

With spiritual sight we can transform fear into confidence.

Exercise for the first chakra

Sit firmly on your chair or on a cushion – and in this body, as though you would slip into a diving suit.

Breath into your Third Eye – hold your breath for a few seconds – exhale and visualize how the energy flows through your body from top to bottom, into the ground and right down to the middle of Earth. Repeat this until you properly feel your feet, the surface below your feet and the energy flow. (5 minutes perhaps. Short sequences will help to keep it playful.)

Our pelvis has the shape of a bowl. Fill it with energy, with your presence and keep your focus in your Third Eye.

Everything is fine if you feel relaxed in your pelvis, calm and stable.

If your pelvis area feels shaky and fretful, you are in survival mode. It is necessary to calm down the first chakra by communicating with it. Unless you are right at this moment running away from something or you have another life-threatening issue, you will make it.

Very often, it is the anxiety of the Body Intelligence we are aware of here. The Body Intelligence mirrors an external situation, responding with shaking or diarrhoea, for example when we witness an accident.

Communicate with your first chakra, and with your body, by saying that you are in safety (I hope that is really true – I do not recommend self-suggestion, which would actually be a lie) and that you, as a being, are ready to take over the responsibility.

The first chakra reacts instinctively when in acute danger. It is not responsible for long-term survival issues. For that purpose, it is better to engage the brain.

Does it feel good when you say:

"This is my body, this is my life"?
Are you standing on your own feet?
Are you ready to take responsibility for your own existence?
Or are you delegating that responsibility?
Is it better if others take care of your affairs?

As far as possible, you should take over that responsibility yourself. That will give you energy and you will, sooner or later, stand firmly on your own ground and no longer on the ground of others – parents, therapists, partner.

As soon as we feel secure, the first chakra will be calm and stable.

Human beings are very different in their feelings of what gives them security.

Find out what you need in order to feel secure – and do not ever forget that one day you will leave everything behind you.

Second Chakra – Hara

The second chakra – the Hara – is located between the pubic bone and the navel.

Element: Water, female quality.

This centre also belongs to the instinctive triad:

1st chakra: survival of the body

2nd chakra: emotional survival and sexuality, symbiosis

3rd chakra: boundary, demarcation of the own space, setting

of limits

A well-fed baby sleeping in the arms of the mother is the perfect image for a satisfied second chakra. The newborn child's needs are taken care of without any effort on the part of the baby. Symbiosis is perfect.

We will better understand the characteristics of the water element by observing the behaviour of water in nature. Water is always flowing towards deeper places, always mingling with every other element it meets on its way. Rain, flowing across the street to the gutter, becomes a brown sauce. The sun evaporates the water and dust is left over.

Similarly, our emotional water element easily blends with everything we meet. In order to avoid getting lost into the "collective soup of emotions", we are well advised to keep our water energy in our own pelvis, not letting it flow out into the world.

Being too curious and using your 2nd chakra energy to feel your way into someone else's energy field, in order to experience everything intensively, will cause you to feel lost, your own energy being stained by all alien qualities.

The sun that purifies the stained water stands for the clear choice of our mind. We can decide for ourselves to what degree we want to get involved and at what time we withdraw from a specific situation.

It is important to realize that we can keep our water element unmingled even in a very intensive relationship or in sexuality. It is as though we would contain our water in a balloon. The balloon can huddle against the other without the energies mixing.

An encounter is always better than mingling and mixing.

This holds in any case true for those who want to walk a spiritual path. Others will often try everything (drugs, alcohol) to experience total blending. To each his own. Tastes differ.

The second chakra and its various conditions:

- The chakra is not used:
  Sensuousness is missing. Such persons usually have a rather "dry" interaction with their own body, with pets, materials, foodstuffs, plants, odours, etc. They seem somewhat stiff in their movements. Sexuality, if at all existent, has a technical or sportive quality.

- The chakra does not have enough energy and/or has been hurt:
  Due to the constant hunger for acceptance, such a person is easily seduced. A kind word, the right compliment and the person belongs to you – ready to be manipulated.
  The needy second chakra follows the programmes:

  "only if you love me,
  only if you admire me for what I am and what I do,
  only if you desire me sexually,
  can I allow myself to be, to exist!"

  The benevolence of others has existential importance.

- The chakra has too much energy:
  There's a high probability that such a person is over-sexualized, always assessing its chances with the counterpart. The person's instincts are developed in such a way that it is always clear who is available and who is not. Just as our neighbours in the animal kingdom.

- Enlightenment of the second chakra:
  It is filled with energy, relaxed and joyful. Sensuousness is naturally integrated. It is enjoyable to smell, to taste, to see, to hear, to touch and to be touched …
  The gait is elastic, one likes to dance and has rhythm in the veins. The sexual energy is balanced and the centre is calm and relaxed.

Sound acceptance and esteem for one's self is a given. One is not dependent on the smile and the compliment of others. It is understood that humans are never perfect and reconciliation with this fact has taken place.

An enlightened second chakra is a source of constant childlike, pure joy that colours everything one does.

Neediness and longing for symbiosis

The emotional neediness of the second chakra hurts quite a bit.

It is the primal pain, the anguish following the lost symbiosis. It may have its origin during birth in this life or already in a previous lifeform.

In his book "Beginner's Guide to Quantum Psychology", Stephen H. Wolinsky describes how deeply the sudden shock of lost security affects us and that we generally feel we are the cause of it. Obviously, this is a non-verbal process, taking place through our feelings. The false conclusion that we are fundamentally not OK entrenches itself deeply. Wolinsky's term for this self-made inner conviction is the "False Core".

Depending on someone's nature, the "false core" statements are:

Something is wrong with me.

I am worthless.

I cannot do.

I am inadequate.

I do not exist.

I am alone.

I am incomplete.

I am powerless.

I am loveless.

Wolinsky maintains that as long as this primal pain is not healed, the purpose of every thought, every action, every project will be directed at not feeling this pain. In order to compensate the "False Core", we create a "False Self" that is as far as possible from the False Core. So we live in a constant compensation, in self-delusion.

Since this is an instinctive behaviour, we cannot grasp it rationally, analytically. We suffer without knowing why.

Relationships offer the possibility to overcome this hurting. We are again lost, confronted with the old suffering, when a relationship falls apart. The false core is confirmed and reinforced.

An exciting sexual life may help to cover up the missing feeling of security. However, it will not be enough to heal a hurting 2nd chakra.

We often meet such "eternal victims". Everything seems endlessly difficult for such needy 2nd chakra persons. They feel unjustly treated. They complain, but they do not see themselves in a position to take their lives in their own hands and to change things. Everything revolves around their suffering. They are always waiting for a miracle. They beg, they pray ... They desperately try to delegate the responsibility to parents, friends, doctors, therapists, gurus, angels, GOD ...

The saying *"Help yourself and God will help you"* is actually meant for such people, but they do not want to hear it. They wait for the help of a magnificent rescuer and often end bitterly disappointed.

Clearly, if we meet someone with an unkind fate, the majority will spontaneously offer support, because true suffering activates our compassion. We give our help so that the person can get up and again stand on her own feet. But we quickly run out of patience if the pleading sounds like: "I am the most unfortunate of all and therefore you have to do ..." Actually, there is a hidden claim to power in such demands.

It happened more than once in my practice that lamenting clients suddenly threw a tantrum because I remained unimpressed by their story. My resistance increases when something is not truthful, sounding too much like self-pity. All of a sudden, the resistance caused the tears to dry up and the client's mind became crystal-clear: the client can now convincingly, without any difficulties, formulate the surging emotional feelings against me. No trace of missing drive ...

To some clients, I managed to draw the attention to their power and their determination just before they angrily left my practice ...

These persons are so used to always repeating the same old story that they themselves are overwhelmed by their power. At least one of my clients completely changed her life after the explosion. At last she assumed the responsibility for her life, changing her job, among other things. Later she let me know how happy she was with her new life.

Moving up from the 2nd to the 3rd chakra is an important development that may generate some unpleasant situations. Doors are banged, swearwords are screamed ... This can be the beginning of a healthy process leading to a new, strong personality. What a waste if the client throws his whole anger at the therapist instead of working on with him. The really exciting work would just start now!

Exercise for the second chakra

Sit in an upright position or lie down on the floor on your back, place your hands on your belly, just underneath the navel.
Your breath flows calmly, the hands feel the movement.

Become aware of the bowl formed in the lower part of your body and bring the water element back to the bowl. The energy of the water element always flows to another person when we blend symbiotically or when we want to feel secure in an emotional field.

Bring your energetic hands (like energetic tentacles), with which you hold onto your children and other beloved persons, back to yourself.
That may take a while because we normally cannot imagine letting go of someone so easily.

Whatever you expect from these other persons, can you give it to you yourself?
For example, the feeling that your life is important? – Can you give yourself the right to exist, in spite of your faults and weaknesses?
Are you capable of being your best friend?

Be your Best Friend!

It is easy to be our best friend on a day when we feel great, when we congratulate ourselves on our success after a successful event.

But isn't it more important to be our best friend when things have gone wrong or when we have to face criticism?

Be good to yourself and give yourself appreciation.

If you have been criticized, find out for yourself what needs to be changed.
After doing so, imagine putting your arm around your shoulders, like a good friend would, because you know:

"It is OK to make mistakes. We do not need to be perfect. I am not going to stab myself in the back because of this mistake."

We walk a path with ourselves. If we betray ourselves and finish ourselves off, then we have no one to walk with.
As soon as we stop criticizing ourselves, our belly will relax and our inner organs will do better work.

Can you already hear the cheerful gurgling of your intestines?

Bring your water element back to your belly. In this way you will become one, instead of only half of a relationship.

And, as already mentioned: an encounter is better than mingling and mixing.

Third Chakra – Solar Plexus

The third chakra lies between the navel and the sternum (breastbone). It is the last of the instinctive triad.

Element: Fire, male quality.

After the baby has spent enough time sleeping in the arms of the mother (water element), the fire element will awaken. The small child pulls away from the mother, gaining more space, in order to see more.

The fire element affects the eyes:

Whoever has a lot of fire, will often feel blazing anger. The advantage of having a lot of fire: a good distance vision.

With only little fire, there is an inclination toward grief and melancholy.
With little fire, near sight is better.

The subject areas of the Solar Plexus are of great significance on our journey. But the corresponding qualities are uncomfortable and are often devalued or criticized. It is definitely not a pleasure to be confronted with people sounding out the qualities of their fire element.

As already mentioned, it can be quite rough when an independent personality is born. Pubescent teenagers and somewhat older rebels give us good examples of how that feels.

Children need the fire. It gives them the courage to say NO when mother says YES. The fire energy allows them to endure the distance to the mother.

During puberty and adolescence, when a lot of hormones and messenger substances are released to initiate new development phases, it often gets loud and fierce. But the new power to be discovered also gives the young people the possibility to take responsibility for their own life and to make clear: "This is my life. I decide for myself what I want to do", while planning to learn "and I don't care what you think of it".

It is sad if this development does not take place. Young people will miss the ability of asserting themselves throughout their life.

I would like to quote Terence McKenna: *"Culture is not your friend. Culture is for other people's convenience and the convenience of various institutions, churches, companies, tax collection schemes, what-have-you. It is not your friend. It insults you. It disempowers you. It uses and abuses you ... Culture creates consumer mania, it preaches endless forms of false happiness, endless forms of false understanding in the form of swirly religions and silly cults. It invites people to diminish themselves and dehumanize themselves by behaving like machines."*

In other words, if you want to achieve something, you will need the power of the Solar Plexus in order to be able to say NO to all standardizing social norms and beliefs that dumb us down, taking or even stealing our time.

Even as adults, capable of using our 5th and 6th chakra to analyse and draw conclusions, it is still the fire of the Solar Plexus that gives us the power to hold on to uncomfortable decisions and to remain consequent.

The fire element allows us to leave the herd behind.

The third chakra and its various conditions:

- The chakra is not used:
  The person is not capable of taking a well-defined position and reacts poorly when conflicts arise.
- The chakra does not have enough energy:
  Such people often remain quiet for much too long. Then, all of a sudden, they explode, screaming things that often have

no relevance to the present situation, only to feel guilty later on, with endless self-diminishing behaviour.

- The chakra has too much energy:
  The choleric person reacts too loudly, too violently, too hard and is very self-centred. With some choleric persons one knows what to expect. Others have a Solar Plexus like a minefield: the explosions cannot be foreseen.
  Things become even worse when alcohol is involved. When uncontrolled anger is acted out, it is to be expected that some quite furious foreign entities have taken possession of the chakra. They are happy to vent their own feelings on any occasion. If someone says "I don't know what came over me. I don't remember what I said and what I did", you can be pretty sure that foreign beings are involved.

- The third chakra is enlightened:
  Those who have worked things out decide for themselves how they handle their fire, and it is not the fire that handles them. Only now do we have the power to take our own decisions. Now we have the opportunity to choose an independent path that is not just the continuation of what family, religion or culture have predetermined.

An enlightened Solar Plexus is soft and powerful at the same time. In such a state, the Solar Plexus serves the heart and the Third Eye.

As a picture, we could imagine a confident martial artist with a black belt. He is relaxed and loving, since he knows that he will always be fast enough to handle any difficult situation. He uses his capabilities to defend or to arbitrate, but never to attack.

Luke Skywalker in Star Wars had to learn just that: *"Never let anger take control of yourself when in a fight."* My quote might not be precise, but the truth in it certainly is.

Handling the fire element

It is decidedly not easy to keep the fire element under control. Especially the male hormones are not designed to deal with hours and hours of computer work, pressing toward aggression, fight and competition. But bears have become rare these days and we no longer build our vessels and log cabins ourselves. Only sportive activities are left to balance out the energetic situation.

Nutrition offers a possibility to influence our fire element: Too much fire can be cooled down with fresh cold water (to drink or for swimming). Cooling foodstuffs such as cucumber, melon, lemon, orange, a lot of raw vegetables, as well as peppermint and sage are helpful.

In order to strengthen the fire element, warming spices such as cinnamon, pepper, ginger, cloves, star aniseed, etc. are recommended. Carbohydrates warm up and so does caffeine, if the body accepts it. Ayurveda and Chinese Medicine provide exact descriptions.

Anger – a valuable asset

Anger is pure life force. Normally, a bit of a rough force and therefore not so popular. But this force carries truth – most of the time. It all depends on how we transform the anger impulse.

Anger, in its purest and most legitimate form, says: *"There's something wrong here. I am not accepting this. There must be a change."*

An impulse for action giving us the power to take the necessary steps. If the Solar Plexus is now let loose, following the first impulse unfiltered, the situation may escalate.

Taking the necessary time to think, answering some inner questions and inviting the heart to take part, in order to evaluate the consequences for others, furthermore exhausting all capabilities provided by the throat chakra, by being creative and perhaps even involving other parties, will lead to a brilliant launch of a wonderful development phase.

It is extremely important to observe what exactly enrages us. It would be good if it were not just hurt vanity. But perhaps it is space and/or border violations, lies in general, lame compromises or abuse – all sorts of untruthful things. Anger is justified here!

Often we experience anger because the world "just isn't the way it should be." And because so many people feel like that and many want to change the world as they please, our earthly matters become dense and denser, tougher and more aggressive...

A patchwork of intentions and opposing opinions.

> *To me personally, to realize that this world is the product of all people on Earth, was helpful to let go of my anger. Where so many interfere, there must be confusion and disorder.*
>
> *My heartfelt sigh: if only people would invest as much energy in untangling, clearing up and resolving matters, instead of adding up more and more ..."*
>
> *But that's how it is: humans want to bring something into being, create, manifest – not the opposite.*

Nowhere else are there more projections than on the level of the Solar Plexus. Who strives for power accuses others of power behaviour and oppression, disorganized people define others as chaotic, liars accuse others of telling lies, those who like to wheel and deal term others as unprofessional. One has to struggle in order to ensure one's rights, thereby joining the others on the same plane. The accusation is near: *"You see, you are always the one to start the fight."*

The best thing is to try to escape from such a situation as quickly as possible! The Solar Plexus fighter will always continue to fight and will never be open to conviction. He will always pull his opponent down to his level. (It is possible to help such people through telepathic work, however, sometimes only after their death.)

It is worth the effort to find out whether the anger is a projected or a justifiable one.

On the other hand, it also happens that justified criticism is rejected referring to the biblical beam in the own eye which is overseen while the mote in the neighbour's eye is criticized. But if every criticism is immediately dimissed, no progress can take place!

Instead of using it for power games, reconciliation with one's own fire and the use of that power to keep one's own projects going will result in fewer and fewer aggressive encounters and confrontations.

Animals and little children love this kind of gentle fire and become very trusting.

That is of course not the slogan of fighters, do-gooders, warriors and revolutionaries. It is rather the message of the mystics who tell you: *"Earth is not paradise, and it will never be."*

Exercises for the third Chakra

In order to release fire, because there is too much of it, sport activities as well as dancing, theatre, games, etc. are recommended.

Releasing anger (by hitting cushions, screaming …) can be beneficial and liberating at certain times. My own experience with "Bioenergetics" (Wilhelm Reich / Alexander Lowen) was important on my path. But this liberating act is a phase that needs to be followed by transformation, understanding, solutions, changes, communication, etc.

The assumption that anger can always be released as described above is wrong. The momentary exhaustion should not be falsely interpreted, because the more we scream out our anger, the more will rise up. The moment will come when we just are angry persons, anger having become our usual state of being.

In order to strengthen a weak fire, a bit of reflection on the value we give ourselves and the value we give this life will be needed. At the moment, this is our only life, even if there have been lives beforehand and perhaps there will be lives after this one. In this life we act, we experience and we learn. Therefore, this life is important.

On our journey, we take with us whatever we have learned. That's all. We do not take our projects. Instead, we take what we learned while busy with those projects. We are not our job, our children, our garden … But we take with us the inner qualities we developed during this life. Is it only anger, then we only take anger with us.

Become the Hero of your Story!

Live your life. It is precious and unique. Live it in such a way that you are fulfilled and satisfied, in accordance with the goal you set yourself. Nobody else will give meaning to your life. This is your assignment!

For you, you should be the central point of the universe (not your ego, of course, but your essence). The same applies to all other humans. You are not their central point, their essence is. Once this point has been understood and internalized, we begin to live our life self-responsibly.

Giving meaning to this life from the perspective of one's essence, i.e. one's Higher Self, implies answering the following question:

"For what reason did this Higher Self, this spiritual being, find it important and necessary to incarnate here on Earth?"

It certainly did not intend to lead a parasitic life at the expense of others. It rather wanted to achieve something significant to improve the quality of conditions here on Earth.

The Solar Plexus stands for the ability to say NO, to be self-determined, to distinguish between what we want and what others want for us. The Solar Plexus is the basis upon which heart love can develop.

Only once we have developed the strength to say NO, can we venture an all-embracing YES from the heart. More on this aspect in the chapter on the fourth chakra.

Welcome the power of your Solar Plexus! It is this power that will also give you the strength and the courage to leave the first triad, the first three instinctive chakras, and to move up to the next triad.

A Useful Metaphor

The personal chakras can be seen as our family

Our second chakra has the characteristics of a small girl. It wants to lean on and to feel secure. It easily feels a victim of circumstances and complains. But it can also be sweet and charming, light-hearted, playful and happy-go-lucky ... It never grows up. And it does not need to. This childlike aspect is part of our being whole.

Our third chakra has correspondingly the characteristics of a small boy. It flares up and fights, swearwords are common. But it will hopefully learn to use its power in a positive way for demarcation purposes and to advocate its projects.

Our fourth chakra has the characteristics of the archetypal mother. Compassionate, nurturing, consoling, patient, kind, supportive ... Sometimes it is too mothering, forcing love and care on others – and feeling used when no appreciation follows.

Our fifth chakra has the characteristics of the archetypal father. Analytical, logical, goal-oriented, creative and determined. It knows how things work and has a hands-on attitude. Sometimes it is too patronising, ordering about. It wants everything to work out as planned.

In this metaphor, the image of a house pet can be used to represent our instinctive first chakra – perhaps a dog?

We live in this body as spiritual beings, taking care of the whole family, pet included.

Fourth Chakra – Heart

The fourth chakra, the heart, is located in the centre of the breastbone.

Element: Air, female quality, the archetypal mother.

A completely new chapter begins here. The heart plays a special role in the sense that, for the first time, we *have here the possibility* to come into contact with real spirituality. The perfect spark of our essence is anchored here, albeit mostly forgotten and covered up with many other things.

We go through many different phases. Perhaps we first fall in love with our parents, have an intensive relationship with a pet, have close friendships with classmates, followed later by the first love relationships.

The heart is by nature sensitive and delicate and it yearns to love and to be loved.

But all of us have also experienced being wounded, losing friends, being cheated on, being lied to and abandoned. That was incredibly hurtful. Exposing the lies of the government or the lies of religion was perhaps even more painful or shocking.

On the heart plane there is much talk of love. In this book I use the term love in a very guarded manner. Sympathy and compassion seem to me to be safer values.

Heart love is sometimes not quite truthful. It is much more of a misty-eyed view, seeing things through rose-coloured glasses. This kind of love does not allow any edges, proclaiming the world would be better if everyone were a bit kinder.

> *Find out for yourself what exactly is meant when someone describes his/her love:*

- Is this kind of love like a sweet sugar syrup that is poured out until the loved one is covered with this gluey substance?
- Or is the love described like a quality of consciousness allowing the loved one enough room to decide as she or he sees fit?

It is often the disappointments and the heartaches that motivate us to take the healing path. The purpose is to heal our own wounds.

The steps are:

At first the heartache seems insurmountable. We see ourselves as victims.

If we are able to contact our Higher Self, we will find out that we are always loved ...

We allow the love of our Higher Self to fill our heart, learning to completely accept ourselves, just as we are.

We do no longer expect others to heal our wounds. The others are busy with themselves and that is perfectly OK.

At last we learn that it is our compassion that makes us soft and powerful at the same time.

And that is the rectified quality of the archetypal mother.

There will always be pain, in any possible situation or form. But pain can result in growth. That is how the diamond is polished. We will learn that it is our "enemies and adversaries" that ensure that the tiniest speck is cleared and cleaned up, provided we accept the challenge.

The most important transformation and reorientation can take place in the heart.

The fourth chakra and its various conditions:

- The chakra is not in use:
  In my generation (I was born in 1950) this applies to approximately 80% of the men and 10% of the women. It seems that the pain endured by men in previous existence forms was so overwhelming that they preferred to protect their heart behind a thick wall.

  In my opinion, approximately 40% of the younger men have access to their heart feelings. On the other hand, approximately 50% of the women have learned to shut down their heart in order to cope with the male dominated business world. However, most of them are able to open up their hearts if private matters are concerned.

  When I was young, I always asked myself: "Is my love sufficiently big?" Only later did I learn to ask: "How much love can the other person withstand and accept?"
  We have to understand: when people with walled in hearts are loved, their protection wall starts to crumble. That triggers enormous fear!
  In order to avoid facing the pain hidden behind the protective wall, such people would even prefer to die or to kill ...

- The chakra does not have enough energy:
  The heart centre is inhabited but wounded and needy. There is a deep longing for being loved and to love.
  Such people always approach other persons but they routinely put the chosen ones to flight because their expectations and hopes are so huge and unfulfillable. Disappointment after disappointment follows.

- The chakra has too much energy:
  Excessively flowing heart energy is found in people with a romantic misty-eyed worldview. They would want to save the world in a childlike, naïve manner: if only people would be kind to each other, if nobody had to suffer pain,

everything would be just fine. The sweet façade is not really credible and difficult to endure. There is a lot of manipulation in such do-gooders. It is a ploy to avoid facing all sorts of challenges and requirements.

- The chakra is overcompensating:
  This overcompensation is based on self-devaluation and is often related to diffuse guilt feelings. So, for instance, it is assumed that terrible things have been done in a previous incarnation, for example during the World War II. So the smouldering wound burdens the heart and the shame about the bad behaviour prevents being able to confide in someone.

  As a consequence, such people try to improve their view of themselves by "labours of love". Gifts, often too many or too valuable, are supposed to give the acceptance they cannot give themselves. Their smile seems warm and sweet, but the emptiness behind it soon becomes visible.

  It is relatively easy to help such people with spiritual work. We either find out that the assumed bad behaviour is really only assumed and we can at last relax. Or, should the assumption be correct, we dissolve karma by doing reconciliation work. The lifelong strains and shadows can be dissolved and freed.

  These empty hearts cannot be filled by the world and therefore many of them project their longing towards a "God", who is supposed to compensate them sometime in the future for their sacrifices and labours of love. Of course, this compensation will also not be given ...

  It is sad to witness such longing ... but until then when we learn to accept ourselves and to fill our own heart with love, there will be no healing.

- The heart level is the realm of give and take. We have to learn that we are not doing anyone a favour by giving too much. And on the other hand, we do not do ourselves a

favour by taking too much.
Our life conditions are different and therefore "too much" can mean different things. (The Higher Self knows what is right.) Giving and taking should be balanced here on Earth. Everything has its value and value cannot always be expressed in currency. Nonetheless, money is often the easiest method of compensation.

We walk a long path with our heart. At least I did so. It needs a lot of courage to dig up the deep pain, to observe it, to cry over it, to ask for forgiveness and to forgive someone. We will have many insights. Our heart will open up so that in future we will be able to encounter ourselves and others warmly.

A warm heart will certainly also come into contact with the pain and the agony of those who suffer or have suffered. The whole suffering of animals, plants, even physical matter, will touch us.

So we will continue our journey ... until we are able to soar above our personal love and find the spiritual love.

- Enlightenment of the heart:
  We do not reach enlightenment just by being happy and loving. Also, even supporting the good and rejecting all bad, we are still stuck in polarity and far away from enlightenment.
  An enlightened heart is purified in such a way that it cannot be hurt anymore, although still full of compassion.

In order to reach this stage, we need to study the deep abyss of the human condition and to understand the emergence of pain and misery.

Those who have been hurt will pass on their own pain, because there is nothing else to pass on. Those who have been vehemently subdued, manipulated and humiliated will also pass this on vehemently. Painful experiences are more strongly remembered than kind, lovable ones and therefore the rate of propagation of the "bad" is higher than that of the "good". That can only be dissolved with inner healing work.

These aspects must be fully understood and considered with all-embracing compassion.

An enlightened heart can be compared to a tree that is firmly and deeply anchored in the ground with its roots. A tree that offers shade, nectar, fruit and oxygen and that nourishes the earth with its fallen leaves. But this tree also started its existence as a seed, became a delicate seedling and had to defy unfavourable weather conditions. It eventually became a young tree amidst other trees giving it protection from storms. It now stands on its own, its turn to give food and protection.

An enlightened heart does not become the victim of victims. But it will always be ready to give a hand to people in need of help.

Emotions of the heart: a roller-coaster

OK, so far we know that compassion and interpersonal love reside in an unharmed or in a healed heart. The heart is however also the seat of the deepest yearnings: we want to love and be loved. When we have at last attained what we so badly wanted, outsize attachments are created because we fervently hold on. So it happens that mothers protect their children who should long since have been released into autonomy. Or relationships that have long since outlived their purpose are not ended. To be mentioned here are also some very curious relationships to pets.

What starts with a claim to possession develops into jealousy, a huge emotional mix of anger, despair, fear of loss and feelings of betrayal, devaluation and abuse ...

The emotional roller-coaster often starts at the heart level and tears us down to the third, second and first chakra. The corresponding healing work is therefore extremely demanding and may last longer than a lifetime.

Some time ago I heard that spiritual beings would envy us for our emotions. In my view, there is no need for such jealousy. Emotions are rather a curse, not a boon. However, I make this statement after 60 years of varied experiences with the wide emotional spectrum.

In order to keep our heart stable and radiant, we will need to do healing and dissolving work repeatedly and for longer periods of time, as well as filling the heart with love. We need to forgive that things are the way they are. This all-embracing healing work is not to be achieved in a weekend seminar.

And no, it is not a particularly exciting work. We take one step after another. No magical tricks far and wide. It is not about a technique, it is about love. And love only "functions" when it is true and honest.

The enlightenment of the heart makes heavy demands on us. I would love to say that it is easily achieved, but that would be a lie.

Fifth Chakra – Throat

The fifth chakra is located at the lower end of the throat.

Element: Akasha, male quality.

Akasha is also called aether and can be equated to consciousness. All four elements earth, water, fire and air come together in Akasha representing a whole.

The "fragments", i.e. the single elements, comprise emotions. However, Akasha is not emotional.

Here is the archetypal father: rational, creative, focused on the external and solution-oriented.

As soon as we use the fifth chakra as window to look outside, we see things very clearly and have many amazing capabilities at our disposal:

- We are rational, capable of analysing and drawing conclusions.
- The fifth chakra can be trenchant. For this reason we are capable of deciding in a fast and clear manner.
- Akasha gives us the creativity to plan and realize unusual, amazing and wonderful visions. We find uncommon solutions to difficult situations. Sometimes, real feats are achieved under stress.
- An unhurt fifth chakra is often in a state of playful lightness and joy.
- We create our own personal expression, our own language, our distinctive signature in this world.
- We find ways to communicate verbally and non-verbally.

That means that we can deliver an unbelievable performance in different areas. Just here is also the greatest danger. The time comes when we feel absolutely great and irreplaceable. A huge ego grows and searches for followers. It wants to be in the limelight, taste the admiration and accept the awards given, while ...

... spirituality slowly but surely disappears behind the horizon.

The fifth chakra and its various conditions:

- The chakra is not used:
  When the chakra is not inhabited, it usually means that a lower chakra takes the lead. It is often women who are reluctant to use this masculine, analytical, clear centre. They let the heart govern and decide, if at all, according to their feelings. The ability to set priorities, to argue objectively and to organise is missing. Such people can easily be influenced by their feelings.

- The chakra has little energy:
  In this case, there is little confidence in the above mentioned capabilities. There is no trust in one's own perception, and no courage to differentiate things, often under the mistaken belief that differentiating means condemning. What follows is withdrawal, hesitation, and making sure one's back is covered. "Better be quiet than to say something wrong!"

  Should you react in this way, find someone capable of giving you an honest feedback and to encourage you. It can be important to find out how others see us.

- The chakra has a lot of energy:
  If highly intelligent, the person will be a fast and clear thinker. Such people are welcome as employees because they do a good job, especially if their heart is also well developed.
  They know how things should be done and how to solve problems – according to their perception. For them, there is

often only ONE possible solution.
Their criticism comes directly and swiftly. That can be of value in a world where political correctness blurs the demarcation line between truth and lie.

- The chakra has a lot of energy, the person has a rather low intelligence:
  The overactive 5th chakra will in this case continuously rattle on, without much reflection.
  However, sometimes even intelligent people jabber non-stop, making a lot of money while doing so ...

- The chakra has too much energy and acts isolated, without any connection to the heart:
  The perception of such people is very precise. They assess a situation very accurately, patronize without being asked for advice and tend to be dogmatic. Conceitedness is a constant danger.

- When the 5th chakra has been fully worked out, all these capabilities are at one's disposal:
  Perception, analytical skills, clever drawing of conclusions, creative expression, precise use of language, as well as playfulness and humour. Such persons are visionaries and often the pulling force in new projects.

  Once the conceitedness has been worked on, they are even capable of letting others take the leading role and/or to accept solutions that do not fully comply with their requirements.

- Enlightenment of the throat chakra:
  The enlightened fifth chakra is at the service of the Third Eye. Because it can operate without vanity, it is an inconspicuous partner. With its creativity, precise perception and communication it repeatedly gives important impulses for discussions and negotiations. With few words it will sometimes avoid an escalation or reactivate stalled dialogues, as well as enrich the quality of the situation.

Little effort – huge effect. One contributes to a situation because something is amiss and not in order to prove how unbelievably clever one is.

Questions to the fifth chakra

If someone frequently suffers from throat aches, it might be useful to clarify the following issues:

- Is there something I do not analyse well enough?
- Do I avoid a clear analysis because I am afraid that I might have to change my life?
- Have I already perceived and understood the issue but am stalling the decision making?
- Am I afraid of possible consequences?
- Would it be necessary to make a certain statement but so far I could not work up the courage to do so?
- Do I prefer to keep quiet for the sake of peace? Am I blocked by the fear of hurting others?
- Is the necessary creativity blocked?
- Is a positive vision for the future lacking?
- Would it be meaningful to exchange views with someone else?
- Would a therapy or coaching be necessary?

Comparisons

Throat and Heart Chakras as a Team

Both chakras work together well provided they are interconnected.

With its clear and fast thinking, the throat chakra on its own can appear a bit hard and insensitive. The compassionate warmth of the heart chakra is just the right combination.

The heart chakra on its own can be somewhat naïve and misty-eyed. Decisions are avoided because one could hurt someone… The throat chakra is the ideal complement.

Solar Plexus in Comparison to Throat Chakra

There is quite a resemblance between the Solar Plexus and the throat chakra.

Both centres are masculine, both are interested in themselves before taking interest in others.

Someone experiencing the world through the third chakra will often come across as defiant, immature, pubertal, fierce, easily enraged, and therefore will not really be taken seriously. The language used is not really sophisticated; swear words being uttered more easily than complete sentences. Stupid comments under the belt are also to be expected. Notwithstanding such unprofessional behaviour, some third-chakra-persons manage to climb the ladder to the management floor, which may result in major conflicts, especially if the subordinate employees are in full possession of their 4th, 5th and 6th chakra.

Someone experiencing the world through the fifth chakra will also first say "I", will have a confident and determined demeanour and know very well what he or she wants. Such a person will be clear and sharp, but not emotional. When feelings run high, this person will hiss rather than scream, will pale rather than go red in the face. Fifth-chakra people are very welcome in leading positions.

The Masculine Centres Resemble each other

First, third and fifth chakras are masculine.

Whether you are a woman or a man, experiencing the world through one of the above chakras will primarily give the point of view of the self. The "I" is the centre of all considerations and sometimes the "I" is expanded to include the family or the employer.

In the best of cases, this will result in trustworthy leader personalities capable of taking efficient decisions and goal-oriented action. Not bad at all for a survival exercise!

In the worst case, these people are unbearable narcissists who unscrupulously insist on all that is to their advantage. All possible shadings exist in between.

If the first chakra is prevalent, the subject is mostly money and yield.

If the third chakra is prevalent, it will be all about status and supremacy.

If the fifth chakra is prevalent, one wishes to be seen as bright, intellectual and superior.

Real compassion and sympathy is not to be expected from such people. But it is quite possible that they have learned certain techniques in order to handle all situations in an objective and precise manner.

For this reason, such people are very good emergency helpers. Speed, versatility, spontaneity and tactics are required in an emergency. Fifth-chakra people are able to work under pressure and they can keep a cool head even in catastrophic situations. If they have learned what is required in a certain situation, they will have the right words at the right time.

Would they open their heart in such an emergency, their capabilities as firefighter or emergency physician would lose efficiency because the situation is just too much to bear.

Some of them try to come to terms with their feelings after working hours. Others are practically not in contact with their hearts, but still render extremely valuable services.

The Feminine Chakras Resemble each other

The second and the fourth chakras are feminine.

Whether you are a woman or a man, experiencing the world predominantly through one of the above chakras will let emotions rule. How do I feel? How does it feel for the others? How can harmony be reinstated?

Such people often have a hard time. When violent conflicts are carried out or painful situations arise, they are overwhelmed by their emotions and are unable to act.

Acting on emotions cannot result in objective decisions because no reliable criteria are available.

In the best of cases, such people have a well-developed gut feeling or heart feeling they can rely on.

In the worst case, they delegate all decisions to others and remain childish. They constantly need a shoulder to lean on. They are very sweet but not really fit for life. They are mostly involved in emotional dramas or even in disasters.

Moreover, people who act out of their second or fourth chakra need constant approval from others for their way of being, thus remaining dependent on others.

The Sixth Chakra – our Third Eye

Our Third Eye is very different from the other chakras.

Element: Akasha, aether. Akasha means consciousness.

One could compare the quality of the sixth chakra with pure light, the other chakras representing the colours of the rainbow.

The Third Eye has whether male nor female qualities.

The sixth chakra is not emotional.

At the beginning of our journey towards enlightenment, we look within TO the Third Eye. Later on that changes: we look FROM there.

The Third Eye is like a portal through which we can access the higher regions, astral as well as spiritual spheres. Or we observe our worldly affairs through the Third Eye and we do this with the objectivity, neutrality and wisdom that are inherent qualities of the Third Eye.

The Third Eye is located in the centre of the head, approximately at the height of the upper rim of the ears – and not on the forehead, as many assume. Holding the concentration in the Third Eye activates both the pituitary and the pineal glands. These are located close to each other in the centre of the head.

If you are a beginner focussing your concentration in the Third Eye, you will notice that its exact position may vary. Always chose the location that feels most comfortable.

This "viewpoint" can also be located outside of the body, a matter of course for those who are often out of their bodies. This technique can be learned and offers a good overall view while also being helpful in experiencing the fact that we are immaterial beings.

Traumatised people (abuse, physical injuries, torture, etc.) usually leave their bodies when in danger. Such situations are accompanied by great fear and it is not always possible for the person to completely re-inhabit the body without therapeutic help. The fears must be looked at and healed. Once this has happened, the person can decide for himself/herself whether to stay in the body or to travel in the astral realm.

For many people, the Third Eye closed during early childhood. For others it already happened during a previous incarnation. These people have therefore forgotten where they come from and who they really are. People with an open Third Eye represent a minority here on Earth. More than 80% of the people are unawake, experiencing this world through their personal chakras below the Third Eye.

But, I also meet many beings who have incarnated for the first time here on Earth. They have already existed for a long time but have been on other planets in this or in another galaxy, or they have been in spiritual realms without any physical coordinates.

They are sometimes called Indigos or Crystal Children. Their consciousness is very free and their connection to the spiritual realms is open. They are wide awake, often multi-talented, but they frequently have no knowledge of the principles applicable on Earth.

I have tried to give guidance to such people in my booklet "STRANDED ANGELS: A handbook for all those who find life on Earth rather confusing.

It is especially such lightful beings who are targeted by astral beings. They have nightmares and during daytime their apprehensions cause fear. The more open and free their consciousness, the heavier the astral attacks seem to be.

Whoever wishes to protect and to accompany such beings during their childhood needs to have a good understanding of spiritual laws and to be well connected in the spiritual spheres.

Many rituals might be likable, dream-catchers and crystals decorative, but in such situations they help as much as hoping and wishing.

Astral powers can only be coped with once you have developed the ability to show yourself in the spiritual spheres in a powerful and at the same time loving way, communicating in an adequate manner.

The majority of the parents have not had the necessary training, so there's nothing left for them to do but to reassure: "no, there is no monster under the bed". And so the children are left alone with their fear.

More details in the chapter on the astral spheres.

The third eye and its various conditions:

- The Third Eye is closed:
  In such a case there is no access to the spiritual spheres. Thinking takes place in the frontal lobe, or in the whole brain, which is also possible without the consciousness of the Third Eye. The intellect is actually just a sub-function of consciousness. The databank, so to say.
  With a closed Third Eye, material aspects have first priority. They seem to be the actual purpose of life.

  With the exception of quantum physics or modern cosmology (for further research see also: "The Electric Universe", "Thunderbolts of the Gods", new findings on plasma, the source element in the universe), both having theories surprisingly similar to the spiritual laws, the generally accepted scientific thinking is far away from spirituality. It is purely intellectual and actually belongs to the fifth chakra.

  Persons with a closed Third Eye and a standard scientific world view can also be influenced by non-physical, astral things! But, what is not supposed to be IS not and therefore categorically denied.

- Ideally the Third Eye is open and connected to all other chakras.

The Third Eye is then the steersman leading a well-rehearsed crew, all rowing in perfect timing. In other words, it is important to aim at our goals with all of our abilities. Each crewmember shares his experiences with the others:

The 1st chakra: alarms if danger is ahead.

The 2nd chakra: makes sure everyone feels well and that everyone gets the necessary appreciation and recognition.

The 3rd chakra: makes sure the crew does not give up and keeps the spirits high.

The 4th chakra: is in charge of all heart matters, motivating all crewmembers.

The 5th chakra: makes sure all have their say, that the compass is set correctly, that the sails are set, the leaks repaired, and it checks the meteorological situation.

The 6th chakra: holds up the idea of the goal, coordinates and leads the team meetings.

All of this is possible and useful in one single person. Each centre is important and makes its unique contribution. Each chakra is to be taken seriously, but we are not to identify ourselves with them. Our goal is to remain centred in the Third Eye and to take all decisions there.

Keeping the above in mind while being kind to yourself, you will learn quite a bit on how to lead a team.

- The Third Eye is enlightened:
Enlightenment in the Third Eye is possible in such moments when all personal chakras are in an enlightened condition.

That means you have experienced the whole bandwidth of qualities, you know when it is too much and when it is too little, you know highs and lows, despair and hope, fear and trust. You have made your experiences, have interpreted and evaluated situations, and you are now (potentially) capable of spotting the congruity and the logic immanent in the game of creation.

You lead a simple and truthful life, you do not seek fame and ego dominance.

The dialogue in your mind has now stopped. You do not think about the future and do not have any regrets concerning your past, emotions are still. Not even a feeling of "*I've made it*" is perceived, which would mean the ego has come in the back door.

Such a moment of enlightenment can be overwhelming. Often the 12th region will open up and we are in contact with Highest Consciousness. We are one with everything that is, an unforgettable experience.

Actually, I should just keep quiet now, because this feeling is beyond words. It can last for hours, days, even weeks.

Let's just pause for a moment and enjoy it.

And: Congratulations! We have made it halfway.

As You Can See, the Book Has not yet Come to an End.

The ecstasy of enlightenment – we do not like to admit it - fades away. It becomes a memory, although we try to maintain the experience alive by all possible means.

Shortly after, we are back in the fangs of life: the neighbour's loud music is annoying; the whining child requires our patience …

In spite of it all, the experience will enrich us. Our understanding of life and creation increases because we can penetrate things with a clear consciousness and with compassion. We will carry on with meditation and with our inner work, and there will be further moments of enlightenment.

The immanent logic of our universe emerges and comes to light.

Consistency and Logic

Oren Lyons, an American Indian eldest, expressed it very clearly: „Nature knows no mercy. Nature only shows us consistency."

It is already possible to recognize this consistency, this immanent logic, from the Third Eye. However, the correspondences and relationships become more obvious for someone looking at this world from a spiritual perspective, beyond the personal view.

It is always the same laws manifesting themselves in ever more different combinations.

> *Whoever has understood sacred geometry, I mean really felt it ... Whoever has taken up the study of the principles of fractals and Fibonacci spirals ... already knows everything. (You will find many excellent articles, graphics and videos on the Internet. It is worth your while to spend some time on this subject.)*

To be in the Third Eye means that we have **overcome** all human emotions. We observe with clarity the dance of the world and the human beings, like an enormous game with faster and slower rhythms, very similar to tides. It is like inhaling and exhaling. Darkness replaces brightness. Tomorrow develops from today. Although everything changes, there are hardly any surprises for the spiritual observer.

By working with all your personal chakras every time you do your exercises, you will notice that the chakras' faculties bundle and work like a well-integrated team of specialists. Each one provides its individual know-how enabling the Third Eye to have a clear overall view.

When difficult decisions have to be made (for example a change of job) it is advisable to consult every single chakra and to put its attitude or position into words. In this way, unclear feelings and concerns can be closely appraised. Taking a decision becomes easier.

The 1st chakra is always concerned with survival and security.

The 2nd chakra would like to feel good and accepted.

The 3rd chakra wants to be challenged, but not too much. Victory must be attainable.

The 4th chakra will look out for friendly team mates and a kind boss. It should feel like family.

The 5th chakra will want to keep an eye on the career. Which capabilities are expected? Are there career opportunities?

These are the concerns of the personal chakras. They are in charge of the physical and emotional requirements.

This has little to do with the meaning of life. It is the self-defined meaning that gives a higher justification. In order to recognise this meaning of life, we will look at our Higher Self.

If such significant decisions are missing, other human beings will make sure we serve their goals.

Development in Three Steps: Thesis – Antithesis – Synthesis

Three steps – at the least – are needed to bring a process to maturity. Sometimes there are repetitions. Generally, though, the steps needed are: "Thesis – Antithesis – Synthesis". These reflect a logical sequence. Knowing this sequence makes it easier to retain the big picture.

Thesis: Who does not move, does not change, remaining stuck in the thesis. One does not want to take any risks. Not moving means knowing where one stands. Quality can never remain the same during standstill. Stagnancy always tends towards condensation, towards descent.

Antithesis: With growing dissatisfaction about stagnation, at some stage behaviour will change into the contrary. This will at least bring movement into the situation. However, the contrary is not necessarily better per se.

Synthesis: After repeatedly tilting between the opposites, one will hopefully be able to evaluate the situation and look for the synthesis.

Synthesis is more than the sum of thesis and antithesis. We rise above the level of the problem and expand the horizon.

Eureka! A quantum leap has just taken place!

Here is an example:

Victim – Perpetrator – Sovereign Grown-Up Person

You have just come home and discover only now that the purchased item is defective.

A. The victim fights from bottom to top:

The "permanent victim" sees the world through the second chakra. With that outlook, we assume that we have been purposefully cheated. Our motto is: "Typical – these things always happen to me!"

We will return the item and accuse the salesman, like a child who has been hurt.

"Victims" wonder that most people impose themselves on them. They do not know that they themselves create this dynamism.

B. The perpetrator fights from top to bottom:

With the consciousness of a perpetrator, we generally look at the world through the third chakra, sometimes also from the 5th chakra.

At some point, most victims free themselves from the hated childish role. The energy of anger and arrogance gives them the power to switch to the winning role at last and with that to become the perpetrator.

That is in fact an important step – however not the highest goal.

As perpetrator we will be condescending towards the salesman and criticize his malicious behaviour or the fact that we have to deal with unprofessional lame ducks!

We are sick and tired of being treated unjustly. We believe it to be our right to be rude!

As perpetrator we aim at forcing our counterpart in the 2nd chakra where he should feel guilty and subordinate.

Such a perpetrator will not accept any obstruction or hindrance, otherwise he or she will be the first to complain about abuse of power.

C. The grown-up person communicates at eye level:

The path from victim to perpetrator to capable grown-up person is only to be attained through reconciliation.

The most important step is to heal the inner self-degradation. Self-degradation leads to subordination or presumptuousness, depending on the actual situation, mood and the counterpart.

We will have to accept that we make mistakes although we try our best. We learn that, in spite of the errors, we can remain "our best friend". A real challenge when having made a mistake. But it is possible – and necessary! That is the only way we will be able to communicate with others at eye level.

People out there in the world have qualities and deficiencies, exactly like you. They (most probably) try their best in order to keep the clients happy (as seen in the example above).

With this in mind, we will take the defective product back to the shop, meet the salesman with respect and find a solution that satisfies everybody. This is also in the interest of the salesman because a happy client will spread the news and will always come back.

Everybody feels comfortable when encounters take place at eye level, i.e. from the Third Eye. For children or grown-ups, patients, handicapped persons, dying persons ... even for animals it is the most pleasant form of contact. We take our counterpart and its issues seriously and can speak of a children-friendly, patient-friendly or animal-friendly contact.

Every New Issue Means Re-Starting at the First Chakra

Life provides us with many possibilities to consciously experience all chakra levels. With every new subject area we again start at the first chakra. It is helpful to know the logic of the steps:

1st chakra: to be or not to be

During the birth process, the first chakra is very active and ensures the best possible conditions for survival of the newly born Earthling.

It feels like "to be or not to be" when you have to take a test, when you have your first date, when you have a stage performance or on the first day at a new job.

Sometimes it is joyful anticipation, or light excitement, sometimes stage fright or just plain anxiety, depending on what you are going through. This feeling can last for weeks, or just for days, hours or very short moments …

Excitement increases the adrenaline level with the well-known consequences: a racing pulse, sweaty hand palms, shaky voice, erratic movements …

2nd chakra: symbiosis – we feel comfortable and taken care of.

The newly born child lies contented in the arms of the mother and sleeps.
You relax. The colleagues at the new job are friendly. You can now switch off your internal alarm system. The situation is somewhat more difficult when we have just fallen in love

because the fear of losing the newly found partner may flare up.

3rd chakra: asserting oneself

Self-confidence increases and we are now in a position to take up room or to defend our space: Children offer resistance, defying and distancing themselves from their parents.

It is those moments when you just don't feel like being friendly, patiently awaiting instructions on what to do. You defend yourself, formulate your criticism and your expectations.

The Solar Plexus likes to use buzzwords. It just requires time until we learn to communicate powerfully in complete sentences.

By being assertive you are questioning the power structure.

Hopefully, you will not get stuck at this level of power and powerlessness, but continue on the path of development.

4th chakra: interpersonal love – self-love

Children fall in love with their parents.

At your new job familiarity grows and you start exchanging intimacies and even start friendships. You give and you receive support and comfort when needed. (Although not all job situations allow the expression of the heart chakra).

Where there is a lot of space for emotions, there is also the danger of suddenly being involved in rumours, intrigues, emotional rivalries and conflicts. From there it is easy to spiral down to the 3rd chakra (anger and demarcation) or to the 2nd chakra (injuries and hurt).

5th chakra: self-expression

Small children paint and create endlessly, they sing, dance and disguise themselves. They learn and improve the spoken language.

You have found out that at your place of work clarity and the ability to discern are more important than heart feelings. So you withdraw your feelings somewhat and differentiate between professional and private affairs.

The 5th chakra can be very efficient, creative, precise, versatile and articulate.

(Beware: do you always interfere, know everything better, always have the last word? That will be interpreted as conceitedness and arrogance.)

6th chakra, third eye: seat of consciousness

Very small children can already have their Third Eye open. Many of them "see" into the spiritual spheres where things can be scary. These children often cry a lot, seemingly without any reason.

Having reached this point, you know pretty well what you can and what you cannot do. It is no longer your most important goal to be in the limelight. You earn appreciation and esteem because you retain the overview, giving valuable tips and related information, thereby increasing the quality of the whole. You assist your younger colleagues with advice and support.

In the professional world there is a constant scramble for the higher positions. But also the possibility of losing one's job is a source of anxiety. People with a strong 3rd or 5th chakra manage to handle this situation best. They take on the challenge, even if nasty methods have to be used. They are ambitious and often the end justifies the means. People with more pronounced 2nd or 4th chakra, whether male or female, have more difficulties with such situations that tend to upset the stomach, increase blood pressure and cause sleeping problems …

Of course, we would all wish to have persons with fully integrated chakras in the high ranking positions in the professional world, as well as in politics. Persons who are mainly centred in the 6th chakra. Such persons would be capable and ready to take responsibility. They would be prudent and be respected by their staff members.

Such a person would also be quite happy with a position at the level of middle management, provided responsibility and appreciation are part of it.

Chakras Are Interconnected – or not

By engaging in spiritual work, we come into a position where we are able to be present in each and every chakra and ever more often – or perhaps even permanently – to look at the world from the Third Eye. Regular mental hygiene exercises ensure a good connection between the chakras or centres. As "captains of our own vessel" we then have the whole crew supporting us.

If the chakras are not interconnected, it can easily happen that a single chakra behaves like a poorly adapted team member, acting on its own and endangering the whole project.

A temper tantrum, loudly throwing our fire energy at the world, can lead to a loss of energy that debilitates us for days, like an emotional hangover. All squandered energy will cause imbalance to our system, sometimes even resulting in illness.

Having made this experience over and over again and wishing to alleviate the situation, you will one day decide to increasingly turn your focus to the Third Eye. That is the only way to integrate all chakras, to collect all observations and information and, having the overall picture, to react in a wiser manner.

If the centres are interconnected, our perception is more precise. We can hold a point of view from "head to toe". Everything flows and is consistent; our YES or our NO is clearly perceived. In this way "our power is with us". Our counterpart will not question us when we communicate with this power:

"In my opinion, it is ...."

"I have decided that ..."

"From now on I will ..."

In order to reach this point, work will be needed. As already seen, every chakra has its own opinion. It is not a question of changing that view by using methods such as suggestion or positive thinking. It is rather a matter of finding our own personal truth, the truth that matches our essence. It is also not a question of our self-will, that ego-centred impulse.

Following the previously used analogy: The captain would hear all parties, collect information, set priorities and then take a decision that can be supported by all crew members.

Gravity Applies to Consciousness

Unfortunately, from time to time, we all go through the same: we busy ourselves with the familiar issues, stay in the comfort zone and are too sluggish to motivate ourselves to learn new things. So it happens that we can go through a lifetime with just two active chakras.

Nobody shows us how we can expand our universe. Perhaps we *do not want* to expand it. Here is a well-known pattern that tends to turn into an infinite loop:

> *Riding on a wave of self-assurance, perhaps after having received a compliment, you inflate your ego taking up more space than you are entitled to (3rd chakra).*
> *Your behaviour is not accepted by the people surrounding you and you are very quickly put back in your place.*
> *You are startled, you may get sick and you sink temporarily in sorrow or self-pity (2nd chakra).*
> *Then, you feel a new surge of energy caused by re-approval and encouragement. You ride on the new wave – until the next blow comes.*
>
> *As you grow older the positive waves become scarcer and the depressive moods prevail.*

Do not give up! It is an art to conquer all levels, to experience the diverse qualities of the chakras and to actually have these qualities at one's disposal. And: it is an art that can be learned!

Like a Staircase, from one Step to the next

1st **chakra:** I want to survive. I take care of myself and my safety.

Danger: We become isolated and our only activity consists of the surveillance of our material goods and the health of our body. It is important to open up and to contact other people.

2nd **chakra:** We belong together. Together we are strong, together we are ONE. We share everything.

Danger: symbiotic togetherness narrows your own area of experience. There is hardly any progress. The emotions of the relationship are the main focus. It is time to focus on the outside. What are other people doing? How can I position myself in the group?

3rd chakra I want to win. I want to deliver a brilliant performance, I want to be right, I want to accept challenges and become stronger.

Danger: We are in a constant competition. The power of the Solar Plexus enables us to draw the demarcation line. We invest in our own projects. We do not care what others think. But the battle becomes epic. The world is full of enemies..

> The transition from the 3rd to the 4th chakra is the most difficult step.
>
> How can we learn that caring sympathy is possible, instead of fearful and aggressive defence?
>
> A new love often serves as bridge ...

4th chakra: We are all in the same boat. We can/should assist each other. This is an important step in growing up. We leave the childish navel-gazing, the self-pity and the egocentric ways behind us and turn towards our fellow human beings with interest and compassion. Now responsible relationships, families can be started.

Danger: Emotions are often overwhelming. We get lost in them and lose the overview. Just in time comes in the next step with its cool analytic expertise.

5th chakra: I show myself with my opinion, trusting my point of view and my ability to analyse. I express verbally as well as non-verbally: that is me!

Here is the place to evaluate what we have learned and experienced and to meet the challenges with our diverse abilities (manual abilities, language, creativity).

Danger: overemphasis of the 5th chakra results in extreme self-portrayal. Some people think of themselves as irreplaceable, they are arrogant, intolerant and patronizing.

They want to do everything themselves because no one can do it good enough and no one knows well enough. They hold all threads in their hands. Partner, children and/or employees cannot make their own experiences.

Is it possible to step back a little bit for the sake of common welfare?

6th chakra: Extra-Personal Observation

Once we have recognised what we are able to do, and once we do no longer constantly need to prove it, we can withdraw from the limelight and give others the possibility to learn, to practice and to be successful.

In the education of children this is comprehensible. In many professional situations this is not possible because many people cling to their positions, or have to cling to their positions for economic reasons.

From the Third Eye (6th chakra) we are in a position to take decisions that serve the whole and are truthful, even if those decisions go against our personal interests.

What is the next Step?

When you are stuck in a specific subject and are not able to find a solution, it is helpful to find out on which level you are. The previous chapters can guide you.

You can also feel inside your body and find out where, in which chakra, there is the most charge.

The mastering of the tools and techniques of each chakra can – but does not have to – take years. There is no way to skip anything. But as soon as you have worked through a level, you can move on to the higher chakra.

Example:

Having been oppressed and devaluated (by mother, teacher, superior), one will spend quite a long period of time trying to adapt, in order to avoid punishment. This adapted behaviour belongs to the 2nd chakra.

Once the energy of the 3rd chakra increases (perhaps through helpful conversations with friends), hurt and resistance will both grow.

At the beginning, the newly found energy will be acted out on its own. The day will come when you feel strong enough to face things and to stand up for your needs. You have arrived at the next higher level, the 3rd chakra.

This also exemplifies that a problem can never be solved at the same level where it arises, i.e. we cannot solve it at the same level of consciousness where we created the problem in the first place.

You may belong to those who, in the face of challenges, react with anger and setting of limits (3rd chakra). For you it is necessary to find out how you can generate sympathy for your counterpart (4th chakra).

Perhaps you belong to those who immediately fall into tears when confronted with a problem (2nd chakra if it feels very childish; 4th chakra if you remain in a grown-up stance at the same time being overwhelmed by emotions).

Such emotions are not helpful in professional life. Your development should lead you to more objectivity. The goal is to be able to react in a grown-up and adequate manner (5th and 6th chakra).

The world does not change – we have to change.

Energetic Communication

If you have read up to this page, you will know that life on this planet is easiest to cope with when you are able to use all chakras unrestrictedly. Once you have developed enough awareness as far as your chakras are concerned, you will be able to choose freely which energies you want to apply in your verbal and non-verbal communication.

When a person's options for action reside in the instinctive chakras, the animal part will prevail. A lot of actions will be knee-jerk reactions. There is not much consciousness involved.

The ability to reflect on something is gained when we use the 5th and 6th chakra. For example, if someone is focused on the Solar Plexus, it will not be possible for this person to understand the arguments of another person acting through the 5th or 6th chakra.

Only by mastering all centres can you speak all "languages".

After having done awareness training, you should be able to adapt in such a way that communication at all levels is possible. This is particularly important for teachers, educators, nursing staff and therapists. They all need to adapt to different levels.

Perhaps the meaning of single words is generally overrated. Obviously, one can use language in a very skillful or less skillful manner. But the most important impression is made by our energetic condition, much before even opening our mouth. Energy communicates immediately and at all times.

We can learn to use energetic communication to provide clarity or to generally improve the quality of encounters. Energetic communication, together with body language, has an effect on grown-up persons and on children, and – needless to say – also on animals.

Misunderstandings do arise sometimes because different cultures interpret the signals in a different manner. Specific training for businessmen with international contacts is becoming very popular. Energetic communication is the most important tool of every well-trained salesman.

But, beware: Misuse is common. In order to avoid helplessness, it is eminently important in our society to be aware of the effect of these energies.

New studies on sociopathy and psychopaths, for example by Robert D. Hare, Ph.D., clearly show that psychopaths have an innate ability to manipulate. With absolute accuracy and in order to reach their goals, they unscrupulously use all means available to them. More on this subject later in the book.

Developing Energy Awareness

All of us are enveloped in an energetic space. Ideally, this space is delimited by a thin sort of energetic skin that clearly distinguishes between "me" and "the rest of the world".

In case you are not yet aware of this energetic space, you can create it mentally. With time it will become absolutely normal to you that our emotional body is covered with a skin.

You can change the size and the nature of this "balloon" at any time. It is well worth your while to play with this idea and to observe how your surroundings react.

- The balloon can be very large:
  That gives a stage star presence - and often provokes aggression within a team.
  People who energetically blow up their balloon to a large size are very quickly thought of as show-offs. Colleagues will try everything to burst the big bubble. Every blunder will be met with malice.
  Adequacy will relax the situation within seconds.

- The balloon can be very small:
  This indicates low self-esteem, fear or depression.
  We all know the mousy persons hardly anyone notices.
  People with a strong Solar Plexus will always react aggressively when meeting someone with a small balloon, because they need a counterpressure to orient themselves.
  If someone is energetically small and hides, they will badger that person as long as needed for a reaction to occur.
  Mousy persons prefer to fall apart instead of raising their voices.

- The balloon is not present at all:
  These people are not properly incarnated, they are hardly aware of themselves and they are easily blown away by the slightest breeze. They are often not really themselves because they cannot distinguish between their feelings and the feelings of others.

- The balloon is filled with fear:
  Fear is easily perceptible for humans and for animals.
  We humans can sometimes even smell fear.
  Dogs tend to attack when they sense fear.

> Meeting a dog with the thought *"Don't do anything to me! Keep away from me!"* often provokes the opposite. The dog comes closer growling because he can sense our fear.
>
> Do the opposite and communicate:
>
> *"I will not do anything to you. You need not be scared of me"* at the same time you keep the demarcation line soft, giving the dog a lot of space.
>
> Not our words are of importance, but our stance. Even if the words are not spoken out loud, the dog will react positively, remain calm and perhaps even come closer to you wagging his tail.

The Journey Goes On

When passing through the gateway of the Third Eye during meditation, it can happen that we find ourselves in the vast endless universe, not knowing in which direction to go.

This experience can be the source of great anxiety, making meditation impossible for some.

In order to dissolve this fear, I hope to be able to give orientation in the following chapters.

First Astral Region: Level 7

Level 7 is very close to the material world. It is, so to say, a neighbouring region.

When our awareness for this level opens up, it can happen that we suddenly have other people's thoughts in our head. To be able to read other people's mind can sometimes be an advantage. But all these banalities are of no interest to you really. They soon become an encumbrance.

It is helpful to definitely decide not wanting to know the thoughts of others and to wait for what is verbally communicated to us. (We will soon learn to verify if the communications are truthful or not.)

Small children often see the beings of level 7 and therefore can communicate very naturally with deceased persons or elemental beings. They are just surprised that not everybody can see them.

On level 7 we encounter all those deceased persons who cannot let go of their body, their possessions. They often show themselves as mental images of their last body, sometimes somewhat younger, with the clothing, hairdos and attributes of their time. Often also they make themselves noticeable through a typical smell: cigarette smoke, lavender scent. Not long ago, I had the visit of a being with a musky smell.

The Hidden People of Iceland are also on level 7. They live in cliffs and large rocks, in a sort of parallel world. At the time I visited them, they showed themselves dressed up in the 18th century style, were rather grumpy and not really communicative.

In my view, they are the approximately 10'000 people who lost their livelihood during the catastrophic volcano eruptions of 1783/84. In those days, the island was practically covered by a layer of poisonous ash. The temperatures dropped worldwide resulting in poor harvests. The Danish King offered to evacuate the remaining 40'000 people to Denmark.

The Icelanders decided against it and held out on the West coast of the island. For many of them, this decision to stay on the island and remain independent had an effect beyond death. The Hidden People can still be contacted today. Sometimes, even streets have to be built around their housing areas because these people know how to prevent the displacement of "their" rocks.

There are also spooks and poltergeist. These deceased people, or people who were killed in a traumatic manner, want to be noticed by all means, or they want to scare the living. Some learn to move objects, to flicker candle flames, or to announce their presence with a chill breath.

Confused deceased persons in level 7 are also found in clinics, where they wait for someone to tell them what to do next, and of course also in cemeteries, churches and chapels.

> There is no need to be scared.
>
> What is needed is people who can offer their spiritual knowledge so that these confused souls can be given orientation and become free.
>
> That is one more reason to read this book to the end and to acquire this spiritual knowledge.

Material Attachments

It would be ideal if we could experience the whole bandwidth during our human life: from intensive body awareness to consciously leaving the body. That would make the shedding of the bodily jacket at death more natural.

When body and material attachments are the most important subjects right up to the moment of dying, then that will not just change after death. In such cases the deceased hold on to physicality as long as possible. That is all they really know. They often remain there where the body died or return to the place where they spent their childhood or the place of an impressive event – good or bad.

Those who believe that "eternal life" means to live on through one's children will hold on to their children's bodies. That can cause a lot of grief for the whole family because nobody feels really free.

Deceased persons can remain in an unredeemed state for an unlimited period of time. Only once they understand the connections and wish to be free do they have this possibility.

Some, however – as I already mentioned – become smaller and smaller through external influences, own decisions, ever increasing karma. Time passes and they expire so to say, falling in a deep sleep, going back to matter or disintegrating.

To send them into the light is no solution. In the astral regions there are many false lights.

But when we ourselves have taken the journey and have experienced the spiritual universes, we can take the deceased beings with us in meditation and show them all regions. Now is the time to drop their attachments in order to become sufficiently free to be able to experience the spiritual qualities. That is exactly what we do during our meditation and so they can orient themselves by watching us. In such a way we can bring them in contact with the immanent enlightened consciousness – provided we ourselves have already experienced it.

This is positive spiritual work which enhances our own consciousness, helps the deceased and enables them in turn to free other beings, for example their own parents.

During your first contact, you can say the following:

> *"I can see you! But you are dead and no longer belong to the physical world.*
>
> *Can you remember how your body died? Let go of your body now.*
>
> *You will have a new body if your wish to reincarnate. You are a free spiritual being."*

Some of them are really desperate and seek help.

Others are asleep and have to be woken up first. Then, there are those who do not wish to be woken up. Perhaps already during their lifetime they had decided to withdraw into silence and are now falling into self-made darkness. And others just want to keep on living their dream, as shown in the next example.

From my Practice

> *A client asked me to spiritually free a wealthy lady. This lady had died in an accident three months ago.*
>
> *I found the deceased lady in her walk-in wardrobe, surrounded by her expensive clothes. She did not see much sense in my offer to visit the spiritual spheres, but after a while agreed to take the guided tour. I did everything to remind her of her divine potential, but that did not really interest her.*

A few weeks later I met my client again. Together we took up the search for this deceased wealthy lady. We found her still amidst her expensive clothes, or rather in her mental picture of her clothes, since these were no longer there.

So much for the assumption that all beings long for spirituality!

Techniques of the 7th Level

Every spiritual level has its spiritual capabilities, but they are denser or more subtle depending on the frequency we are in contact with.

Clairvoyance

As soon as the awareness for the 7th level opens up, we can suddenly find ourselves having other people's thoughts in our heads. The ability to read other people's mind is not as cool as one would think. Most of the thoughts are trivial. – As mentioned at the beginning of this chapter, it is helpful to protect oneself by taking the corresponding decision.

A person whose consciousness resonates with the frequency of the 7th level is capable of perceiving matter. That person can see distant places and events, can say where lost items are to be found, can diagnose a displaced vertebrae in the body, can see gallstones, etc.

A special branch of clairvoyance is called "Remote Viewing" (important names in connection with Remote Viewing are Ingo Swann, Russel Targ, Ed Dames, Courtney Brown …). It is a precisely defined technique that leads to amazingly good results. This ability is of special interest to the secret service, but also of course for the study of the time and space phenomenon or the study of the various functions of awareness.

The technique as such is neutral. The question is of course, who is interested in the results? Persons with special talents in this area are very important to the secret service and the military. These persons become state property as soon as their talents are discovered. It has become well-known that in America children are tested for extra-sensory abilities at a very young age and, in case they have special talents, they are specifically trained. Free will and self-determination are not foreseen.

Flying and "Astral Trips"

Both are possible at all astral levels.

On the 7th level we travel with heavy luggage. One sort of rolls out of the physical body, taking a lot of energy with, making it possible to become visible in other places or even to touch other people. These then believe the "astral traveller" was physically present. (Robert Monroe has done intensive research and written books on the subject.)

The higher the frequency of our consciousness, the more subtle is our way of travelling in the spiritual realms until we eventually reach spiritual consciousness and develop the ability to be everywhere at the same time.

The Frequencies of Level 7 Have an Effect on Matter

During moments of stress or intensive emotions, people who are tuned in on the frequency of level 7 will cause surrounding matter to react. For example, lightbulbs or glasses may explode without having been touched or clocks and electrical appliances may switch on and off.

If your computer starts reacting to your energy frequency, trouble is ahead. Our everyday appliances are not (yet) so developed that they can be steered mentally. But we can assume we have this capability within. We might even have used such capabilities in other places before. Our planet Earth is not home to the highest developed lifeform in the universe. Some of us carry memories of previous existence forms. And sometimes these earlier capabilities peep through causing problems because our world is not compatible with those capabilities.

It also happens that astral beings occupy and influence an electronic appliance. Simply because there are too many beings and not enough bodies. Astral beings choose to inhabit machines thereby causing annoying disturbances. Sometimes the astral beings choose to inhabit objects that are admired or venerated, such as sacred images or statues. All of this can cause quite a bit of confusion.

Someone with good spiritual abilities can free the astral being and return things to their normal order.

Healing

Persons having a good ability for communication with matter will quite naturally develop capabilities that are beyond the normal. Such people often feel the urge to become shamans or healers.

The majority of healers and shamans of both genders are active on level 7 because, in order to influence matter, they make use of energies closely related to physicality.

Some of them also have access to level 8, where they "feel" and influence the emotions and energetic dynamics of relationships.

They generally do not have access to level 9. It is rather so that they are dominated by beings of level 9.

I know that I am stirring up a hornets' nest with this statement because healers and shamans have a high standing in our society. Let me explain.

This creation game has been brought into being by all of us together and we certainly all have a right to make experiences here for as long as we wish to. There is nothing wrong with that.

However, there are quite a number of people who are convinced that they have made enough experiences or have suffered enough and they do not wish to continue living in this limited reality. They feel as prisoners and the thought of reincarnating in this world is anything but promising.

In addition, some of them carry memories of free, more subtle spiritual realities in their consciousness. For them it is clear that they need to do everything possible to avoid reincarnating. They want to become free, if not immediately then at least after death.

This book is about clarity. I will explain why some techniques only enhance our prison and fail to free us.

In this world we often busy ourselves especially with material manifestations; busy with our own body, with possessions in all their forms. Methods to improve our life here on Earth do so through the frequencies of levels 1 to 9. The methods are not really wrong. We should just not believe them to be spiritual. If you want to remain in this world and are not interested in freedom, you are most welcome to use these methods. Those who want to become free have to choose another path. You will read about this later in this book.

Spirituality (levels 10 to 14) is beyond. This is a differentiation, not an evaluation. We need to understand that those beings in the spiritual levels do not have the intention of changing the game. Would they have such an intention, their frequency would immediately densify and they would find themselves in a denser universe, i.e. in the astral realms.

Having intentions, wanting to change and manifest things is totally another state of being, of energy, than resting in love, being compassionate, just being. "Spiritual healing" does exist. It has a completely different quality. More on that in the chapter on level 10.

Those who exert influence with their own power and resoluteness, in order to clear away symptoms, must always expect an echo coming back to them. That is a physical law: energy goes – energy returns. Healers working with this energy have no insight into which karma they are taking responsibility for and what are the consequences.

In order to really be able to heal, we need to have an all-embracing point of view. A craving for harmony and not being able to bear up against pain are by far not enough.

As long as the instinctive chakras 1 to 3 are not cleared up, the consciousness frequency will be heavy and dense. In this situation, access to the astral realms is possible, but not to the spiritual levels. That is a very limited sight. People in this situation are easily seduced, especially when fascinating astral capabilities are demonstrated.

The instinctive issues have to be understood, cleared up and healed before the journey can continue.

Dealing with one's sense of superiority, i.e. the personal conceitedness, is quite a challenge here …

Not all healers influence the energy with their own power. Very often there will be astral helpers interfering and using the healer as channel. That complicates matters in a way that cannot be understood, whether by the healer nor by the patient. The latter two are only concerned with recovery. But the issue is much larger than that, the consequences can be immense, perhaps even beyond death.

There is a tangled mix of suggestion, hypnosis, placebo effect, energies, good intentions, bad intentions, power, manipulation, exploitation, dependence, belief, confidence, hope. Moreover, there are the astral helpers, by no means divine entities, who like to bring the persons involved under their control.

The whole subject of healing is much more of a complex issue than generally assumed. Disillusion commonly sets in a few years later (my critical comments refer to "wonder methods" such as Reiki and other forms of so called spiritual healing. They do not apply to therapeutic techniques such as Shiatsu, lymphatic drainage, Rolfing, Cranio-Sacral Therapy, Feldenkrais, etc. These techniques can give good results without any astral intervention). A very clear awareness is required in order to discern what is going on in the background and what is going wrong.

Unfortunately, the "pact with the devil" is common. In the chapter on level 9 you can read more on this subject. You will certainly recognise the truth in the statements of the spiritual mystics:

> *Spiritual mystics basically advise not to use occult powers and not to give them any importance. Siddhis – the so-called occult powers of levels 7, 8 and 9 – are diversions. They are spectacular, call attention and seduce the ego. They have no spiritual value and put us into (karmic) trouble.*

In the spiritual realms we are going to learn much more valuable contents. You can confidently leave the Siddhis aside.

Yes, I know, that sounds like a lot of work.

Our prison planet is extremely well guarded. The grid is fine-meshed. There is no back door and no easy getaway into freedom.

We will only be free once we have again become what we really are: pure, spiritual beings. For the majority of us, it is not an easy but with certainty a rewarding path.

Stop! What Happened to the Crown Chakra?

You may think I forgot to mention the crown chakra. I did not.

In my own model, which has proven to be very useful in many years of practical experience, the 7th chakra is the crown chakra, the first chakra of the higher section. So the 7th chakra belongs to the astral realm and is not enlightenment.

Believe me, it took a long time until this became clear to me!

That does not mean I disregard the valuable qualities associated with the crown chakra. It is just a matter of a different order.

This realization is based – among other things – on the following experiences and observations:

- In my perception, the programmes that give distinction to the gender-related, social, cultural and religious behaviour and thinking become visible on the skull cap.
  Some people have right here a comprehensive script, a notion of how life should be. These people are always standing just a little aside of real life. They do not really feel themselves and will not spare any effort to turn their inner images into reality.

- Gopi Krishna described his period of suffering in the book "Kundalini". By concentrating on the 7th chakra, Gopi Krishna had aroused the kundalini energy and directed this energy in the wrong direction. It took months for him to get a grip on his life again. A very dramatic report.

- Mystics with a pure consciousness are not interested in astral subjects. They use the Third Eye as gateway and get directly into the spiritual spheres. That is why they give the impression that the spiritual spheres are just "behind" or "above" the 6th chakra, naming the spiritual spheres 7th chakra. They are actually in the quality of level 12.

- The pineal gland (Corpus pineale), generally associated with the 7th chakra, is practically at the same height as the pituitary gland. Concentration in the Third Eye activates both glands.
  Since the pineal gland is the gateway to the spiritual world, the healthy condition of this gland is of vital importance. (The synthetic sweetener Aspartame – in NutraSweet, AminoSweet, etc. – is involved in the calcification of the pineal gland. The sweetener is added to sugarless products and medical drugs although safe alternatives would be available. The manufacturer of Aspartame was taken over by Monsanto.)

- By concentrating on the skull cap one reaches the lowest astral region, i.e. "Johnny's Paradise". I gave it this rather derogative name because all the conceptions, desires and phantasies, such as young maidens pampering us after death, tables covered with exquisite meals, ... are placed there.
  People also often imagine a "paradise" where flora and fauna are intact. Everything should look just like on Earth, but be perfect. No murky rivulet, no withered tree, not even the animals devouring each other but living peacefully next to each other.
  The dream of a world without problems is an illusion we create ourselves. At some stage, we will wake up sobered from this dream, very probably in a new incarnation, and hopefully having recognized that the biological reality is different.
  The fact that the stronger one swallows the weaker is necessary. It starts with the microorganisms we carry in our intestines, on our skin, in our lungs. Without them our life would not be possible.
  And, what happens at a low level continues to happen at the level of animals and humans.

Those who create astral illusionary worlds will land in those worlds after death. Most of the deceased and astral beings are grateful when we communicate with them and show them the way back to their real spiritual essence. They have long ago forgotten the knowledge on this subject. They need help from outside.

Without assistance they will remain in the astral spheres until they eventually incarnate again. Reincarnation is directed by karma and has little to do with free will.

To believe we could get help and assistance from deceased in the astral spheres is an illusion. They are still biased and trapped. No one becomes wise or even holy just by dying. On the contrary, it is the deceased in the astral spheres who need our assistance to become free.

Second Astral Region: Level 8

Level 8 resonates with the second chakra. The themes of level 8 are therefore clear: longing for symbiosis (feelings of security and belonging) and sexuality. This region is an immense universe – and at the same time, a well-known pitfall on the spiritual path. On level 8 everything is so cosy, so secure, perfectly matching all emotional longings - at least at the beginning. What could possibly be wrong with that?

The Possibilities of Level 8

Astral trips:

Astral trips are possible in all astral regions. On level 8 we travel per emotional energy; with the sexual desires and longings or with the desire to belong somewhere.

At this level, "belonging" always means partly giving up one's divine perfection in order to meet the given criteria of the level. Level 8 games let us very quickly forget our spiritual potential.

Diagnostics:

As soon as we get acquainted with the frequencies of level 8, we will be able to "read" the emotional qualities of others. "Reading" means here being aware of. Many have a sort of gut feeling or inner knowledge. This feeling is in most cases rather vague. I would recommend practicing this "reading"-capability, for example by asking your Higher Self to give you a picture.

We can "read" the quality of a relationship: are the participants respectful, affectionate, understanding, on an equal footing, dependent, abusive? We can recognise what is taking place between the participants on the emotional level.

Most clairvoyant persons (mediums) "see" into the levels 7 and 8, or let beings from these levels pass on information to them. Their clients are mostly interested in issues concerning health, money and relationships.

For the clients, the source of the information remains hidden and is often erroneously interpreted as spiritual. They are right in the middle of the illusionary astral world. Spiritual beings have no interest in readings or prophecies. Whether the information received applies or is helpful, apart from raising hope, is a completely different question.

Healing:

Healers who work in level 8 influence the emotional energies.

Becoming dependent is a considerable danger because level 8-healers also satisfy their own emotional needs and want to be nourished. That is one of the reasons for working at this level.

These "astral magicians" will always use the energies in a manipulative way. The temptation is just too sweet. Without the need for power and manipulation, these healers would not be found here at this level.

And: the ones who feel attracted by such strategies are also needed. The seductive look of such a charismatic level 8 healer is just unmatched. No one else would be able to see so deeply into our souls … The healer's voice is melodious, hypnotic and seems to enchant. Many seekers have travelled around the world to have such an experience.

Those people who have a sort of affinity for "miracles" are in danger of being seduced. If necessary, the miracles will be invented – after all it is all a matter of interpretation.

Many have a deep distrust or even a profound aversion towards the methods and particularly the energy of level 8, which feels like a thick gluey syrup. They feel that something is not right, not truthful.

In the chapter on level 10, I write on spiritual healing.

In order to attain their goals, astral magicians also like to place pictures, information, emotional impressions in the energy field of the manipulated ones. These people then have the feeling that

- they knew the magician / this person in the past
- they have karma in common
- or even shared incarnations (the corresponding pictures are delivered at the same time ...)
- they are meant for each other.

That is how people are entrapped. They feel they have just met an old friend. Such an opportunity to learn more about oneself, to experience the cosmic determination should not be neglected – so they think. And, obviously, they cannot imagine anything more divine than having sex with the magician. The magician's goal is achieved because this bond holds; unless the victim has effective spiritual tools to dissolve the bond.

"False Gurus", more concerned with their egos and not so much with truthfulness, prefer to work from level 8, and they even do so if they have the capabilities of level 9 (which is rare). They prefer to disguise themselves with a sweet, seductive surface, which brings them more success. Would they openly show their level 9 capabilities many would just flee. Level 9 capabilities are only used when the gurus want to spread fear. This applies to incarnated humans as well as astral beings.

Note: "Guru" is the Sanskrit word for teacher and is a neutral term. It has become common practice in the Western world to use the term guru to disapprovingly designate teachers using improper methods.

Emotional Desires

Many think and hope that their burning longing for a loving community, for belonging and for warm emotionality should be fulfilled at least in "Heaven".

There you go: in level 8 they find a cosy nest. (We always land first in our own dreams.)

Should you, after having gone through the earthly disappointments, be searching for the wonderful Big Mama who looks after you, or the magnificent Big Daddy who knows everything, there is great danger you could get entrapped by the corresponding astral illusions. In order to prevent that, it is generally useful to check on the state of the 2nd chakra and to get it into shape.

The goals are:

- to learn to be your best friend!
- to nourish and heal your emotional neediness with self-acceptance,

thereby creating a strong foundation which, to a certain extent, helps avoiding the traps of the illusionary promises of level 8.

But even with an enlightened 2nd chakra it is possible to have astral longings and to enjoy being seduced in one way or another. The temptations are varied and the ones of level 8 are particularly sweet and promising.

Spiritual beings can serve as an example so we can learn to discern the differences in quality. Unfortunately, such beings will not show themselves in level 8.

Many deceased remain for hundreds or thousands of years in level 8, respectively they again land in level 8 after each incarnation. For them it is not possible to find out who they really are and how to tap their full potential.

Astral beings of level 8 generally show themselves in an angelic outfit. They master many techniques and tricks and know exactly how to impart awesome experiences to the longing: sweet shivers, cold and hot, feelings of enormous expansion, melting into a perfect one with others, overwhelming joy, sexual arousal right up to ecstasy ...

These terms cannot but give a glimpse of the qualities of astral interactions, which are considerably more impressive than anything we can experience on Earth. It may feel like a drug we are not willing to miss, and also because we have the impression that a direct connection to "Heaven" is being established ...

No wonder passion is in the eyes of those who have experienced this level. It is the well-known radiance of some New Agers ... Can such feelings be a lie? The feelings just have to be true if they touch so deeply?

Nevertheless, they are illusionary. These feelings create bonds, dependence and are diminishing, and therefore have nothing to do with spirituality.

It is the "Sweet Hell" of Lucifer's amusement park in its best manifestation, run by suppressing powers. The gentle angels suddenly turn into dark demons as soon as one tries to escape from their kingdom. The hurdles that need to be overcome should not be underestimated.

Only once we have experienced the downside of dependence and being totally at somebody's mercy, do we realize that the qualities and criteria of spirituality have long been lost.

We now need someone at our side having already walked the path to spiritual freedom.

Do not forget that your liberation is possible and that you are entitled to it.

Astral Sexuality

It usually begins harmlessly. Our lover is not nearby or is already dead. We are full of love and longing, and we concentrate our full attention on the other being. Longing is like a magnet through which beings are attracted to each other.

First astral contacts normally take place during sleep when censorship is switched off. After waking up we believe we had a dream. But the encounter was real, even if not physical. The other being was really present with his energy body, which is relatively dense on level 8.

It is not always possible to determine who took the initiative. The encounter is the result of a mutual agreement.

We feel the embrace, the kiss or even the sexual interaction – exciting, ecstatic or caring, consoling, healing.

This is the nice version: two people/beings who love each other and wish to have an encounter create such a meeting in the astral spheres. It can be a fascinating experience and, as long as only the two lovers are involved, it remains a manageable game.

However, there is a danger of astral powers getting involved and the lovers lose control of the situation. The emotionality opens a door that is difficult to close if one does not have spiritual capabilities. So, very quickly the game turns into a serious pitfall.

The same door is also opened when we act out our sexual lust in phantasies. You are wrong if you believe that thoughts are "free" and that you have the right to involve other people in your own mental-astral-erotic phantasies. A mental sexual assault is felt as irritation by the counterpart and has the same karmic consequences as in the material world.

Additionally, such mental activities are an easy target for astral beings. They intervene, heat up the emotions and passions until the participants lose control of themselves. After all, the astral beings feed on these energies.

The astral beings leave traces in our energetic body in the form of sparks of awareness which can be activated at any time. People are then very surprised when they feel sexual lust so-to-say out of the blue.

> Astral beings will always try to push and transcend the boundaries and to drive human beings into unkind, devaluating, illegal or even criminal acts.

As already mentioned, the same thing is also done by human beings. Any conceivable emotion can be aroused through the use of electronic frequencies.

Strong ethical paradigms can protect us to a certain extent. However, it must be stated that modern mind control techniques are stronger than an ethical stance.

The frequencies are strong enough

- to let us think exactly what the powers want us to think,
- to let us feel what they want,
- or to let us act the way they want us to act.

The above is a statement by Barrie Trower. He is an expert on microwave-warfare. You will find his speeches as well as documentation on this subject on the Internet.

This fact is difficult to bear up with! The further our mental and spiritual capabilities are developed, the greater our possibilities to withstand such mechanisms.

Useful Information on Astral Sexuality

Some people have absolutely no affinity to level 8. I do not know the reason for this. But I do know for sure, that life is easier if the door to level 8 remains closed.

Only a few have enough spiritual knowledge to be able to come out clean after a walk on that level. Effective techniques and if possible someone who supports and accompanies the process is needed.

The energetic space also remains protected when two people in a reciprocal love relationship and with an intact trust in each other are together. It is helpful if both partners decide to protect their love.

In spite of that it can happen that astral beings cling on, or that we resonate with emotional fields that make us rougher.

Clear your energetic space regularly.

The clearing of the energetic space is of special importance after sexual interaction – not because your partner or sexuality as such is dirty, but because astral beings or sparks of awareness can easily jump in.

You can comb through your energetic field and dismiss all foreign sparks of awareness in your system. At the same time you take back to yourself everything you spread out in the world (longings, attachments, all sorts of emotions).

Know that every sexual lust can be caused from outside.

- It can be that you go in resonance with signals in advertisements and films.
- It can be the energy of the 2nd chakra of another person that brings your 2nd chakra in action.

- It can be that someone tries to influence you through level 8, consciously or unconsciously.
- It can be an astral being interested in sexuality.
- Or it can be electric frequencies (Mind Control) that are supposed to manipulate you.

If you go through a period of time without any sexual activity, you will make interesting experiences as far as sexual energies and their dynamics are concerned. You will feel much more precisely what exactly influences you from the outside. Moreover, the quality of your consciousness will change because your body energies need to organise themselves in a different manner. A really exciting and rewarding experiment increasing our independence and self-determination.

It is not my intention to be a poor sport!

Every single being is absolutely free to enjoy each and every astral amusement, to fathom all capabilities and gimmicks, and to satisfy every curiosity. Many do exactly that for very long periods of time. Only those who grew weary of all these games are motivated to leave this realm behind them.

I write for those looking for spiritual freedom and enlightenment, and who are therefore interested in clear discerning criteria.

There are few such beings, therefore precise information is of utmost importance.

How to Recognize a Truthful Teacher?

For millennia there have been people who have attained spiritual perfection. There is no need to re-invent the wheel! We can profit from their experiences and our own personal path will still be an individual one.

Unfortunately, quite a few teachers wade in the same swamps we want to leave behind us ...

The Logical Question Should Be:

How can we recognize whether someone is capable of assisting us on a truthful path?

The media inform us about black sheep, egomaniacs, narcissists and psychopaths who endanger the life of their students. Those are exceptions. The great majority gives its very best.

Unfortunately, sometimes the very best is not good enough! We only see those dimensions we are aware of. Perhaps there are others. Moreover, even an enlightened being may not be the best teacher for every student, at any given time.

In spite of that, I would like to list some of the discerning criteria I consider to be important:

- Truthful teachers support their students so that their personalities can resonate with their own spiritual essence.

- It is more important that students learn to trust their inner voice than to obey the teacher. Truthful teachers lead you to your own autonomy and not to dependence.
  Try to find out: is the teacher doing everything him-/herself or does he/she teach you to become capable yourself?

- A true teacher will not boost your ego, i.e. your vanity. Teachers who do that want dependent students.
  And just because true teachers do not give importance to the student's ego, those looking for splendour and glory will soon run away.
- True teachers meet you at eye level.
  It is not their goal to dominate others or to groom their own reputation and image.

Ask yourself the following questions concerning your teacher:
- Are you aware of an attitude of giving or rather of an attitude of taking?
- Does the teacher serve the purpose, the path – or does the teacher serve himself?
- Do you feel free – or do you feel manipulated?
- Painful experiences can also help you on your way. Read what happened to me:

A long time ago, I had a teacher who could manipulate me energetically in such a way that my heart chakra opened and flooded him with love.

For an astral magician this is no big feat. He was successful with his method and was therefore surrounded by women who were manipulated just like me. He could give you the feeling of being the chosen one.

Interestingly, all these women resembled each other: they were pale, docile, humble and submissive ... This is the kind of students found surrounding many false gurus. Tirelessly they nourish him with their adoration, admiration and love.

I have learned, and today I can recognize hungry energy vampires from far away.

This lesson was very painful – and at the same time very important. No person is either all good or all bad! I also learned enjoyable and constructive things I still apply today – and I experienced painful things. Looking back, both were beneficial on my path.

- True teachers do not want to be put on a pedestal and do not allow their feet to be kissed, whether physically nor metaphorically. Not only do they not like to be on a pedestal, they also do not want their students to diminish themselves.
- True teachers are in contact with the spiritual essence and see this potential in their students. In such a way the encounter at eye level can take place.
- Those who disavow the existence of very powerful and destructive beings have not yet encountered the challenges of the astral realm.
- Those who try to pacify or to oust the "bad spirits" with magical attributes and rituals obviously cannot themselves rise above the astral spheres.
  A spiritual person having the necessary knowledge and all-embracing love can stand up to such beings.
- The truthful teacher will teach you all of this, in accordance with your own capacity and speed.

Dependence through Admiration

Students sometimes glue their admiration on to the teacher.

Admiration is heart essence; it is like gold leaf that we paste onto other people. Clearly, we can hardly separate ourselves from such people because that would mean cutting off a part of ourselves.

In relationships based on admiration, we feel subjected, emotionally dependent and often not really grown-up – not a good feeling.

This type of relationship is often promoted by false teachers. The dependence and the gap created by the admiration are not really favourable to the learning process.

In case such energetic dependencies exist, perhaps the relationship to your first love or to an idol, you can proceed as follows in order to dissolve them:

Understand that the leaf gold consists of sparks of your admiration. It is your heart essence.

If you glue your sexual lust onto someone else, that is your energy of your 2nd chakra.
(You already know it: if your energy is pasted onto something out there, you are not free!)

Take back the sparks that belong to you.

That may sound pretty abstract, put it will happen as soon as you have understood what it is all about and have decided to do it.

If it worked, you will definitely feel the difference:

You will feel equal because you are no longer placing the other person in a higher position.

The idol has become a human being – without any gold plating.

Appreciation and esteem for someone else is absolutely OK. We carry those feelings within and they feel good. But as soon as we admire, energy flows to the idol. We thereby diminish ourselves.

Some idols have got used to this additional energy. It is food for their ego. *"Great! They all cheer. I am just unbelievable!"*

On the other hand, there are artists who attract attention by being unassuming and simple. They seem to be resistant against admiration and that makes them endearing.

Recommendations and Rules

Be especially careful when your emotional reactions towards someone else are out of the ordinary.

Remember: emotions can be created to impress you and to make you dependent.

Never consider emotions as a proof of truth. Check out the same situation the following day. And again the day after. And again the following day ...

Oh yes ... I know, it is not easy.

What we have experienced and understood ourselves, we can be aware of in others.

Third Astral Region: Level 9

The universe of level 9 is enormous and encompasses innumerable intermediate levels and hierarchies in which smaller and greater "gods" reign. Right on top are those beings who are not programmed by others, but who have decided to be programmers themselves. They are so powerful that at the beginning they will not even cast a glance in our direction. We first have to prove to them that we are to be taken seriously.

However, it can take years before we meet them. They will only appear once we have become so strong with our spiritual work that we (might) endanger their game.

But since everyone in level 9 blows himself up, we soon have the feeling that our counterpart is very, very powerful. With time and practice we learn to recognise the subordinates, who have themselves been diminished and programmed. Only the ones right on top of the hierarchy decide on their actions.

So there are innumerable hierarchies, different games and an endless number of beings. When these beings attack us, they sometimes appear as frightening devils. It can also happen that they do not take any shape at all, but their energetic presence is so scary that we panic. The body goes into a state of shock because it can feel that it could be destroyed within seconds.

Magic, manipulation, secrets and lies are everyday tools for the level 9 beings and with those tools they generally achieve what they want. They openly show their superiority and chose the most promising disguise in order to impress or to frighten their counterpart.

Very important: never forget that you are a free spiritual being. They are not YOUR gods if you do not give them entitlement.

If You Have Been Frightened by a Level 9 Being

The first thing to do, should such a being frighten you - it will generally happen during a dream from which you wake up with a racing heart – is to take a step back.

Withdraw from the contact! Gather all your concentration back to you and make sure you become whole.

Take your time, move around, take a sip of water, find your inner centre.

Contact your Higher Self and place your feet firmly on the floor.

Only now are you ready to contact that being at eye level and calmly explain your rights to him. You can tell him:

I have the right to be here. And I have the right to be free. This creation belongs to all of us. You have no right to dominate me.

This is the short version, the first-aid-measures so to say. You will find more on this subject in the chapter on freeing beings.

Our incarnation in a rather fragile human shape has detached us from what we actually are. Out there in the universe, there are beings who do *not* identify themselves with a biological body and, compared to us, they are immensely strong and capable. At the beginning that is naturally really scary!

Not all of those beings show themselves in a humanoid shape. There are also reptilian, aquatic, insectoid, feline and other shapes for which we have no names. In contact with such beings, it is difficult for humans to maintain the trust in their own power.

Through spiritual work we are reminded of our capabilities and at the same time we come in contact with beings that have never lost this knowledge.

It is of value to have someone on one's side who knows how to deal with these beings. We can ask questions and learn, because we have to become capable of confronting these beings with consciousness and power. A power struggle would not be the right approach.

Meditation will equip you with whatever is needed for these encounters.

Contact a professional should you want to understand what exactly happens in these realms and how these events could be surmounted.

How the "Gods" Define their Game

- We govern. The others obey. They are our slaves.
- We decide. They are the subordinates.
- We have the right to decide for others. This right is ours since the beginning of time.
- We are superior. The others have no significance.
- We judge and we punish. The underdogs must be trained and drilled.
- All of this is our right. It is our game and consequently we make the rules.
- We are gods. No question about that. Therefore, the others are not gods.

"Gods" position themselves beyond all questions at the top of the hierarchy.

How Spiritual Beings Define their Game

Spiritual beings make similar statements. However, they mean something completely different:

- I do not govern, I create. I create a game and all who wish to participate are welcome.
- I decide for myself. The others decide for themselves.
- We decide for the ones who cannot decide: children, handicapped or unconscious persons no longer capable of deciding or acting for themselves.
- I do not feel superior, but I am aware of my divine nature. This divine nature is in all of us, without exception.
- I teach, instead of punishing. I promote an understanding and, especially, I am an example.
- Within the game, we are all part of a continuous process. We take the responsibility and give our best.
- We are all divine. Divinity is pure love for all and everyone.
- We stand for truthfulness. Discernment is necessary for truthfulness!
  We do not serve the interests of power and we do not support any conceitedness.

What We Need to Know about Level 9

All beings in level 9 want power. Of course, they come from the same Source as all of us. However, the level 9 beings at the top of the hierarchy are here because they want to be here. They enjoy their enormous influence and want to see it increase continually. They want to triumph and master. They do not act out of pleasure and joy but because they want dominance. To attain their goals they use all instruments of power to their full extent.

The fact that they achieve this, i.e. that they want this, means that they have negated the spiritual and have opted for power instead of compassion and love.

Powerful rulers in level 9 have followers. The followers may have chosen their role freely. However, the majority of them just believe that they have decided freely. They do not remember how they were programmed and hypnotized into being slaves.

Actually, the large majority of all beings in the astral spheres are subordinates who unquestioningly support the power pyramid. They do this for a sense of belonging, which allegedly gives a meaning to their existence. Also, they hope to be upgraded one day, allowing them to escape from the power game. Unfortunately, they will be promoted to a dead end, at best. They are on a downward spiral and not on the upward one.

In case you feel all of this is not really new and that it also seems to happen in our world, it is no coincidence. It is the logical continuation of our worldly game in the astral spheres. Very few realize how programmed and enslaved we are. This game has been wonderfully engineered.

Cold-Hearted Psychopaths Rule the World

It is important to understand the astral events and their connections because the same things happen here on Earth. They are just somewhat downsized, playing out one octave lower, so to say.

Human beings who are right on top of the earthly power pyramid, generally not in full public view, are connected with level 9 beings. They do not struggle with diminishing feelings such as shame or repentance. They do not know such feelings.

They have enormous amounts of money and pull the strings in the global power play. In order to gain access to coveted natural resources, they drive less developed countries in the debt trap, forcing them to render the exploitation rights of their resources.

(John Perkins' book "Confessions of an Economic Hit Man" is a must read.)

Indigenous groups are killed, rain forests cut down, oceans scrupulously polluted and fish stocks depleted. Genetically manipulated trees are planted, palm oil or soya are cultivated where once natural forests thrived. These monocultures harm the land. Chemicals are sprayed in the skies to manipulate the weather – and possibly also for other reasons.

The list of exploitation and destruction of our planet is very long. The question is:

"Why do these human beings, whom this power has been given, destroy our planet? What is their motivation?" The most common answer nowadays is: *"Because they are psychopaths. They are unscrupulous and seem to enjoy the pain and suffering of others. Or they want to greatly reduce the world population."*

The discussion on the subject of psychopaths is in full swing, especially in the U.S. In everyday language, and in the public opinion, the term psychopath is mainly used to refer to serial killers such as Hannibal Lecter in the film "The Silence of the Lambs". A series of authors and studies (Robert Hare and Paul Babiak, Kerry Daynes and Jessica Fellowes, Jon Ronson, Martha Stout, Thomas Sheridan and others) have shown that psychopaths are found on all levels of society and in all professions. The psychopath can be our neighbour, mother, father, child, partner, work colleague or boss ... Many of them have had contact with justice at an early age, or would have had were they not such good liars. But not all psychopaths are murderers.

Nevertheless, psychopaths turn life into hell for their environment. It is very difficult to remain sane and healthy in the presence of a psychopath. Relatives and colleagues often become depressive. Burnout and even suicide are common reactions to the accusations, exploitation and unfair treatment. In order to avoid breaking down, many develop themselves psychopathic traits.

In a world where greed, boundless consumerism and wastage lead to success, psychopathic traits are virtually bred.

In their book "Snakes in Suits", Robert Hare and Paul Babiak described the general criteria of these relationships and created the term "Corporate Psychopaths". These are the psychopaths who manage to reach key positions in a corporation, in order to obtain the corresponding compensation. They seize every opportunity for sexual adventure and, especially, they create further opportunities in order to profit financially from the corporation, even going as far as driving the company into bankruptcy.

This new definition of the term psychopath has not yet reached the mainstream media in our geographical area. Unscrupulous people are described as "ambitious", "spoiled by success", seldom as "narcissistic". For me it was an eye-opener to read about the precise new definition. I find it important that more people learn about it because psychopaths control world affairs.

Characteristics of successful psychopaths:

Psychopaths can be males or females. The ratio lies at 50%. According to U.S. surveys, 1 to 4% of the population are born as psychopaths. (The author Thomas Sheridan warns that innate means incurable and that you should run away from psychopaths as long as you can. Psychopaths are very destructive - and infectious.)

Psychopaths have an elevated Testosterone level. They are driven, permanently looking for the next kick. That makes them venturesome. They take quick and sometimes surprising decisions. At least in the beginning, they seem very convincing.

Psychopaths use their intelligence to accurately observe and analyse their counterpart. They then activate those traits of their personality that will appeal to their counterpart, enabling them to take advantage of the weaknesses of their victim and to successfully manipulate it. Psychopaths are notorious liars and perfect chameleons.

You will find psychopaths in all social classes and in all professions. Needless to say, corporate power and international finance have a special appeal to psychopaths. The greed for big money coupled with approval and acclaim is a dangerous mix. Thanks to their confident demeanour, psychopaths obtain positions of power within a corporation, often without a critical examination of their C.V.

For many superiors, the charismatic, adventurous, charming, well-groomed, eloquent applicant seems to be just the right candidate.

Psychopaths always feel superior. Their audacious behaviour is impressive. Psychopaths stop at nothing, are ruthless and uncompromising. They will unscrupulously put out rumours in order to damage someone's reputation.

The past life of psychopaths is generally obscure. Their stories leave a disturbing feeling that something is not right.

Psychopaths are often involved in various relationships at the same time. They are emotional parasites, looking everywhere for what serves them best. In order to create a profitable nest for themselves and to ensure professional advancement, they will also enter into marriage and beget children, whom they will not really care for ...

Before their scams are discovered, they have already moved on.

The brain of psychopaths works in a different manner. When shown images of suffering and violence, the normal brain will react with a firework of signals. The brain of a psychopath remains practically still. The brain activity is restricted to the reptile brain. Psychopaths have no empathy. They do not have the slightest possibility to empathise with suffering people or animals. Shame and remorse are unknown to them.

The Decisive Interface between the Worlds

The interface or gateway to our world is to be found there where the powerful beings of level 9 and the psychopaths meet. In my experience, unethical, unkind, egocentric, destructive or manipulative behaviour is always supported and reinforced by astral beings. That makes it so difficult to cope with such behaviour.

Surprisingly, during my investigations on the subject of psychopaths, I often encountered the opinion that psychopaths actually do us a favour because only thanks to them can we develop our strengths. As a consequence, we learn to observe attentively, to take clear decisions, to network, to become really creative and innovative, etc.

Yes, unfortunately! Based on my own experience, I can only support this opinion. My unwavering trust in the inherent perfect core of humans, prevented me to place a NO when necessary, and I failed to set a demarcation line in time.

In the polar world there are always both forces. Their only purpose is for us to grow.

And this Is How Level 9 Beings Operate

Level 9 beings always find a way to manipulate human beings like puppets on a string. It would seem they possess a tool enabling them to amplify emotions, transmit pictures, intentions or even orders, in order to attain their goals. But, astral beings do not need tools for such a purpose. They have the ability to influence energies directly. (Humans have instead developed many tools to influence frequencies. These are the "non-lethal weapons" of modern warfare. The corresponding healing tools such as Radionics, MindWaver, and others have a much weaker effect.)

In their role as highest gate keepers, they make sure humans remain trapped in the Earth orbit. Sometimes they even force other beings into a specific incarnation so that they remain prisoners in "Lucifer's Amusement Park" - to use this sloppy expression.

The astral level 9 gods have the following areas under their control:

Banks, Insurances, the complete Financial System
Chemical and Pharmaceutical Industries, Bio-Tech
Healthcare
Entertainment Industry
Radio, TV, Press

Electronic Communication, Social Media
Schools, Universities, Education
Military, Secret Service
Politics
Religions
Organized Crimes and Illegal Drugs.

The astral powers will not let anybody get away with anything of importance.
Their governing motto is: "Divide and Rule".

The System (the Matrix) is everywhere. But, of course, there are also well-meaning, dedicated and good people in all listed areas and branches, who sacrifice themselves and try their very best. They simply cannot imagine that the goal of the top management would be to constantly increase control.

Only the conformists are rewarded by the System. Only they may be successful. Our mental and spiritual freedom is the price we pay for the social security offered by an employment.

Conformists are those who help to spread the lies of the System and who do not question the System openly and publicly.

And that Is the Reason Why

- Children are vaccinated, in spite of side effects and subsequent illnesses
- Drugs are tested on uninformed patients
- Seeds are genetically engineered, in spite of the fact that none of the grand promises by MONSANTO and the GMO Lobby have proven to be correct
- Results of studies with negative outcome where rats developed serious tumours after being fed GMO-foodstuff are suppressed

- Seed propagation on a private basis will soon no longer be allowed

- Nuclear power plants are declared profitable, in spite of the fact that the costs for final safe disposal of nuclear waste products (whatever that may amount to in view of half-life periods of a few thousand years ...) and the costs for dismantling have not been included

- Waste products of nuclear power plants are processed into munition and used to contaminate war zones, to destroy the genetic material of the population and the planet

- All sorts of data are ruthlessly falsified

- "Traitors" are silenced. When ridiculing and threatening do not help, family members or the "traitors" themselves will "commit suicide", meaning that they will be murdered in such a way that the mainstream press can present it as a suicide.

The ones who do real good are spat out by the System. They remain unsuccessful and do not obtain the necessary funds. Or a reason is found to bring the person to trial.

Living on this planet makes it impossible to remain completely out of the System. The net is getting more and more small-meshed, monitoring and slavery are on the increase!

You can develop an effective healing method.
As long as you remain in a small circle, in the back room so-to-say, you will be safe. If your method is really good and gains recognition, you will soon be slowed down and subdued.

The Powers will not allow any affordable, natural healing methods. (An example: "Cancer – the Forbidden Cures", on DVD or on YouTube http://tinyurl.com/kg6ldq2)

For the same reason, some of the EU-countries have forbidden growing medicinal herbs in your own garden, e.g. sage. In

France, important fines are imposed on those who promote stinging nettles as medicinal herb.

Plants with a natural resistance to pests are squeezed out or forbidden. Seeds of plants more prone to diseases are a lucrative business. (See also: The Primeval Code - Electrical Fields instead of Genetic Engineering.)

The list of those who have developed and those who still work on "free energy" devices is long. Many have been silenced with large amounts of money, others have been murdered …

Fact is that still no such device is freely obtainable on the market. The Powers are interested in keeping us dependent on fossil fuels as long as possible. So the CO_2 taxes and all other sorts of taxes and duties can still be collected.

> It is important to wake up.
> We are losing our freedom in large chunks.
> The psychopaths are in power and it is very difficult to escape from their control system.

Once more, in Order to Avoid any Misunderstandings

On Earth, we very seldom meet human beings who operate with level 9 capabilities.

A person who bawls at you is probably doing that from the third chakra. The roar always seems somewhat childish.

If someone finishes you off without getting loud, he is probably doing it from the fifth chakra or from his intellect (a sub-function of the 6th chakra). This person will bawl you out and try to make you feel like a child.

Level 9 really feels more supernatural. One could say infernal. Usually, the person talking is not really your counterpart but a level 9 astral being who is taking advantage of the situation.

> You will notice that the situation has to do with level 9 because your energy will react in a completely different way. In "normal disagreements" with human beings your energy remains intact.
>
> The encounter with level 9 will easily pull the rug from under your feet and you will feel that effect for quite some time.

Try to look through the person you are dealing with! Become aware of what is going on behind the scene and treat this being as described in the beginning of this chapter "If you have been frightened by a level 9 being".

That was quite a chunk. High time to make a pause and to remind ourselves of who we really are.

Let Us Taste the Sweetness of a Short Meditation

Spiritual meditation carries us away towards a completely different frequency.

Spiritual love heals our fears. We rise above our anxieties and disappear from the "control radar" of the astral gods.

It is my pleasure to take you with me, across the stream – from the astral levels to the other bank, in the spiritual worlds …

If you want to cross a stream, you will look for a steppingstone in the middle of it, in order to jump and land safely on the other bank. In meditation the landing place is called LOVE and COMPASSION.

And here are the steppingstones on the way:

- You may be sad because you have not felt the enchantment of spirituality for a long time?

- Allow the sadness to be for a while. Sadness will transform into yearning.

- Be aware of that yearning. What exactly are you yearning for? For peace in your heart? For the magic of bliss?

- All these qualities are already within you. Just keep at it, contemplate that yearning, allow the movement of flow and allow the transformation to happen.

- Yearning can turn into gratitude.
  And there are many reasons to be grateful:
  You remember your spiritual nature, your spiritual home. The majority knows nothing about it and have long been lost in programming, conditioning and emotions.
  And I am sure there are plenty of other reasons for being grateful.
  Gratitude is very close to love.

- Are you aware of the small light in your Third Eye and/or in your heart? Enjoy the "spark of love" within, care for it and nourish it. The spark reflects your essence.

- Love your love and it will multiply itself.
  Your love will nourish you like nothing else can.

- This is the way from sadness to yearning and through gratitude to love.

- Find the way from hate to love.
  It is feasible!

- Find the way from desperation and hopelessness to love!

You can discover all these ways. And you can walk the path step by step. It becomes easier with every time you walk the path.

The gate between level 9 and level 10 is like the very small eye of a needle.

If you do the exercise described above, you will imperceptibly leave everything behind. Just by concentrating on something else. And that exactly will free you sufficiently to make it through the eye of the needle.

Enjoy it!

* * * * * *

I will now rest my head of my pillow, melt into the bliss I described above and stay there while my body sleeps.

Good night!

* * * * * *

More on Level 9: "The Pact with the Devil"

There is much more to say about level 9. For example, it is important to talk about alliances. These are frequently formed as a result of innocence or ignorance. I have therefore chosen this dramatic title ...

At the end of the film "The Devil's Advocate", the devil, brilliantly starred by Al Pacino, says with a malicious smirk: *"Vanity... is definitely my favourite sin"*.

The devil knows how easily humans are entrapped and how difficult it is for them to let go once they have become deeply engrossed in something.

They often realize much too late that they are on the road to ruin. How many roulette players still believe in hitting the jackpot, although they already have gambled away house and future.

Vanity easily attaches itself to fast money, luxury and status. They are obviously door-openers to higher circles, whatever the expectations ...

However, it is also vanity and conceitedness when someone refuses to adapt and does not accept any instructions. Of course it is important to be able to think and act for oneself. It is just as important to be able to follow instructions and to adapt to the situation at hand. We want to be whole human beings. That includes characteristics that oppose each other, i.e. that complement each other in the polarity.

Those who meditate can just as well succumb to vanity. That would be the case, should one hear a small voice saying *"I am so unbelievably enlightened!"*

The next day already new challenges are presented. We are forced to decide and to act.

And in the meantime, we have learned that every decision, every action and every omission has a positive as well as a negative effect. And that is exactly the reason why there is no such thing as "I have made it!"

Vanity demands the differentiation: "I am better than you – you are not so good". Or even: "I am good – you are bad!"

Feelings of conceited superiority create antagonism, injustice, rivalry, deceit and struggle. These are exactly the games that astral powers love and which they support because they reflect their motto *"divide and rule".*

> *(Important: There is also a compassionate superiority. It can be seen when someone feels strong enough to accept responsibility, to organise and manage things and to lead.)*

The astral powers enjoy the inclination of human beings for conceitedness. It gives them innumerable game possibilities and they can be creative.

But their most important hold on human beings is fear.

Fear is easy to poke. Fear makes us feel small and discouraged. Out of fear we accept exploitation and are prepared to give up our inner conviction, step by step, in order to maintain a narrow comfort zone.

Medicine and Pharma diligently fuel this fear because anxious and scared people are a good source of money. So they make us believe that physical and emotional health is only to be attained through regular check-ups, medical interventions, vaccines and medicaments.

Traditional knowledge on how to lead a healthy life is suppressed and declared as superstition. At the same time, the superstition that chemical drugs can do more than merely combat symptoms is declared as a reality.

In the Diagnostic and Statistical Manual of Mental Disorders (DSM), the net is also getting tighter. No matter what people feel or go through, it is a disorder. So, even the fear of actively addressing unknown persons at a party is declared as a disorder that needs treatment. The condition "healthy" does not exist!

There is, it seems, a pill for every condition. And there is also a pill for the side effects of that pill, respectively another pill for the side effects of the pill against the initial side effects. So it is not uncommon to find people with three different prescription drugs. As a consequence, people are not really getting any healthier, but business is good and anxiety is on the rise.

We now also know that the medicaments and hormones patients eliminate through urine cannot be satisfactorily filtered out of waste water and therefore are reintroduced into drinking water. Do I need to give more details ...?

Unfortunately, ever more people prefer to take happy pills instead of learning to deal with their emotions.

How is the Pact with the Devil Initiated?

In moments of fear or in order to achieve ego goals, people tend to solicit the help of spiritual powers and that is how the pact with the "devil" is made.

Some people might say: "But I am entitled to divine assistance!?"

That is exactly how the ego shows its greed, its pretension. And that is exactly what astral powers wish to hear. They will certainly offer their assistance. At the beginning they generally also deliver fantastic results in order to consolidate the pact.

However, after a while, dependence comes into play. Business is slow, losses have to be accepted, related parties run into dangerous situations, one's reputation is endangered, physical power dwindles due to disease – and nobody answers one's imploring prayers.

Those who have chosen to walk a spiritual path will be tested on all subjects:

- The fear of losing our good reputation and our credibility (3rd chakra) is closely related to vanity, susceptible to blackmail.

- The fear of losing a loved one, one's own children or the best friend (2nd and 4th chakra) makes us emotionally vulnerable.

- The most difficult situation is when our own life is in danger (1st chakra). It is the fear of death.

These challenges have to be met by:

- Learning that we cannot please everybody. But we may rely on the fact that many people have enough intelligence not to believe all rumours.

- Becoming, as far as possible, emotionally autonomous and striving to stand on one's own feet instead of living a symbiotic relationship. Every human being has its own life story. Claims of ownership are not helpful.

- Learning to integrate death in one's life plan. Spiritual meditation helps to surmount this difficulty.

In this way, our adversaries and challengers become our best and also our most severe teachers.

We have to understand: Except for the right to incarnate here on earth, nothing is due to us.

What we receive from our community is a gift. Our community grants us an advance. It invests in our future because well-educated children will in turn (hopefully) contribute to the wellbeing of society as a whole.

To make it very clear, let us state once more: we have to pay dearly for our stay here on Earth in form of setbacks, disappointments and losses. Naïve enthusiasm is often brutally destroyed and we are left with empty hands.

It is commonplace that it is exactly those experiences that take us further. But even that does not happen automatically!

In order to grow from these experiences, they have to be evaluated and they have to go through an alchemical process, so to say: the accumulated pain that burdens our heart and feels like a lead weight needs to be transformed into gold. That requires time, commitment, intelligence and dedication. Otherwise, we will just grow older. Wisdom is not available free of charge.

Just then when the pain seems unbearable and we carry the question within *"Which perspective should I take in order to understand what happened with more wisdom and all-embracing love?"* can our consciousness open up to an understanding that did not exist before in our mind.

So, let us go back to the "Devil" whose intent it is to maintain the power game with as much subordinates as possible, in the greatest possible realm.

Astral alliances can hold their validity for a very long time. Sometimes their validity cannot be measured in earth years. Whichever way these pacts were made, a change can only become possible once the beings decide not to be enslaved any longer. Hopefully, they will then find a way out of the pact.

Not knowing how real freedom, perfect and enlightened consciousness feel, it is difficult to ask the right questions. It is therefore helpful to have a good guide. To have someone who knows how these astral pacts function is generally indispensable. It is difficult and it is the reason why so many human beings remain the prisoners of self-appointed gods.

The masquerade of these self-appointed gods is so perfect that even their existence is questioned.

The most dramatic pacts I have seen, i.e. those involving one-sided dependence, were generally related to spiritual healing. Many of these healers have a huge ego (vanity), assuming they have been chosen in a way or another.

The promise to be endowed with powerful healing energy through a method, such as for example Reiki, is difficult to resist. With their consecration they are given access to the huge astral Reiki energy pool. This energy gives force to the method.

In the meantime, it has become known that this method is not completely harmless. The pool is carefully managed. Whoever takes from the pool has to refill it. That generally happens after death when the beings become prisoners of this astral game – and that is the end of spiritual freedom.

Dependence or Freedom in Healing Work

I do know, of course, that the majority of spiritual healers have only the best intentions. For them it is simply inconceivable that a divine being, i.e. a well-meaning "God", should not have as much compassion for suffering human beings as they themselves have. They therefore firmly believe that their work is good without exception. They do not have the understanding that "divine" involves everything. Real spirituality does not evaluate, does not differentiate between good and bad, has no opinion as far as good or bad is concerned and does not have preferences, does not prevent and does not support either. All these aspects belong in the astral realm.

Healing work that uses exterior spiritual energies guides the patients' attention in a wrong direction:

- Dependence is created.
- The belief in an unseen power that is not understood is encouraged.
- The responsibility is delegated to astral "heavenly powers", thereby making us smaller.
- The patients fail to take over responsibility for their situation.
- We fail to learn the language of the body.
- We fail to make best use of the illness by seeing it as a challenge to grow. How can we then experience our inner wholeness?
- We do not learn any self-healing techniques.
- Often, the idea is created that divine mercy needs to be earned. No wonder patients feel disappointed or angry when divine mercy is not delivered, in spite of the sacrifices to earn it.

Spiritual Communication Is the Key

Being able to communicate spiritually changes everything and is of elementary importance in any kind of healing.

Communicating does not mean wishing, requesting, asking or praying. Using too many words can often cause confusion and is usually ineffective ... Effective, spiritual communication is something completely different.

Spiritual communication consists mainly of devotion. We meet our counterpart with a loving, comforting attitude, go very near and at the same time offer plenty of room. Our personal opinions, deductions, prejudices, fears or concepts do not have any importance at this time. They would disturb the process and our clear awareness in many ways. So we leave them aside.

In healing, we generally communicate with cells. This happens without words.

> *Open you heart and be with whatever is. Go very close while at the same time offering plenty of room. In such a way you will become aware of things.*

The cells will show you their emotions and pictures. Sometimes they will show traumatic accidents, sometimes surgery that has confused them ... Through our compassion they can eventually let go of their trauma and return to a better functioning.

Do I need to explicitly mention that this method does not only prove successful with cell consciousness?

We *are* consciousness and we communicate with consciousness. It makes no difference whether our counterparts are a group of cells, foodstuffs, matter, animals, plants, children, adults, deceased people, nature beings or aliens.

However, beings have different sizes. We have to adapt ourselves so that communication can function. That is easy. Size is not really of great importance. It is more like air with which we fill a balloon, a bit more or a bit less.

The rules for good communication always remain the same:

- We never work without the explicit consent of the counterpart. That would be interference and reflect a "know-it-all-attitude".
  When I work with clients, I inform them verbally. If the beings I am working with are not physically present, I inform them telepathically that I am prepared to assist them with their ailments and problems. I only work with them if they so

wish. They generally feel relieved and cooperate willingly.

In the telepathic communication, the beings see me in my wholeness and immediately recognise that I have no intentions to manipulate or to act destructively.

- I never give instructions to the cells or to the Body Intelligence. I give them my support just as I would give it to a being.
- I respect their free will.
  Everything that has consciousness has a right to free will. If we have something positive to offer, it will be welcomed with enthusiasm.
  Pressure, even if very subtle, will always create karma.
- The secret of the therapeutic process is the vacuum
  – because pain and suffering cause (excess) pressure. Counter-pressure is not helpful. I offer a room for the pain, the shock, the fear, the helplessness and the confusion of the cells.
  I do exactly the same with the beings.
- I now listen to what the cells have to tell me, of what happened to them. So, I sort of listen to their worries. This communication is non-verbal. The cells show me their pictures and their feelings, i.e. their complete inner film.
- If the contact is empathetic and warm, the consciousness (of cells, Body Intelligence or beings) will feel it has been understood, will relax with a sigh of relief! Even a beginner can feel that clearly.
- Only now do I offer different methods. The cells will chose what they need to heal. The chosen 'remedy' can be:
  — A regression, if the trauma is in the past. The trauma has to be carefully looked at, in order to rehabilitate the healthy state that existed before the trauma.

— A remedy such as a wet pack, cold or heat treatment, herbs, homeopathy, vitamins, minerals, etc.

— The cells will tell what is abundantly present and what is in deficiency.

— The cells will tell whether there are intolerances, e.g. to ingredients in foodstuffs, toiletries or in the environment.

> The purpose of this communication with the cells is to enable consciousness to properly handle situations, questions, disturbances.
>
> And: truthful healers do not wish to be amazing magicians.

In general, spiritual knowledge will be needed to solve and clear a situation. However, in our day-time consciousness we do not have access to this knowledge. Who would know exactly what is needed so that a broken bone can grow together again? But we can contact this knowledge.

This blueprint knowledge is available in the spiritual realm.

All these techniques need practice. The communication with the cells and the Body Intelligence is not easy, but certainly rewarding. The best way is to practice with little aches and pains such as colds, headaches, small cuts and bruises.

Of course, there are situations that require emergency treatment with conventional medicine. It is too late to practice at such a time. But we can still assist the healing process with spiritual communication, and we will be surprised by the speedy recovery after accidents or surgery.

Each successful recovery will increase the confidence in one's own communication capabilities.

Allopathic (conventional medicine) drugs suppress symptoms and interfere with the natural body functions. That may be necessary at certain times. However, the Body Intelligence is never excited by such propositions. Once we get used to letting the Body Intelligence have its free will, merely offering our support, we will also find, in most cases, alternative ways for the healing process to take place.

Good Communication with Cells and Body Intelligence Is the Basis for Healing!

And it will also help to deal gently with the dying process.

A few healers manage to stay free or to become free. They are the ones who have understood the spiritual principles and who act in accordance with these principles.

They have left vanity behind them, staying connected to their spiritual essence. They accept death as a possibility and they take back their personal wishes, not promising any wonders!

That attitude is exactly what removes the landing strip for astral beings.

The astral powers will tempt us right there where we have egotistical pretences.

Gratitude will save us from the ego trap.

Liberation of Beings

From a worldly point of view, walking a spiritual path makes us feel increasingly lonely because the possibilities for an exchange of views become increasingly rare.

However, at the same time, our spiritual world becomes populated by evermore beings who try to come into contact with us. We attract these beings like a flower attracts bees.

As soon as we develop a spiritual presence, we become visible. You will have to get used to this situation. Therefore, it is absolutely essential to learn to communicate with these beings.

I am inserting this chapter here because these beings (ancestors, deceased, disoriented, etc.) are to be found in the astral realm.

Additionally, there is a given urgency, because I do not want them to scare you out of your wits. It would be a real pity should you leave the spiritual path as a consequence of such encounters.

Later on, once you have walked the path right up to the Numinous, you will handle such situations with competence and poise.

> *Before going on, here are just a few indications:*
> *First of all, you should get a general picture of the situation and read the description of the spiritual realms and levels. Make sure you have internalized the qualities of the spiritual levels.*
>
> *Study the themes of the levels, meditate ... and you will be able to follow the steps described here.*
>
> *Sooner or later you will be able to resort to this information and hopefully apply what you have learned in a matter-of-fact manner.*

Let's Go

The prevalent belief is that we should protect ourselves from astral beings because they are evil and dark. For this purpose, mostly magic means are implemented: ghosts are banished with holy water or a crucifix, they are smoked out or ostracized. The most absurd means are used, there is a lot of superstition involved and one is taken back to the Middle Age ...

Others send the beings "into the light". That is not really helpful when there is only a vague notion that light is equivalent to good.

I do not banish anyone nor do I send anybody anywhere. I show them what I know and what I have experienced. The confirmation that this knowledge is helpful comes immediately. Previously evil, angry or devaluated anxious beings return to their original innate quality, showing their radiant, unburdened and relieved nature. After liberation, their feedback is clear and unmistakable. They are very thankful for the knowledge about their real essence.

We ourselves can immensely learn and grow from these encounters. The so-called evil beings are ultimately our best teachers. With their attacks they show us where our weaknesses are and where we still have work to do. So, unintentionally, they make sure that we really attain spiritual perfection.

> By the way, evil, destructive beings do not like to hear that. After all, their aim is our hindrance, not our development. That is at least the case as long as they themselves are not free.

And we learn a lot about the spiritual realms, because the beings we liberate share their stories with us.

In the regular spiritual meditation you will learn to discern the various levels. Earnest spiritual work (perhaps with someone's assistance) will deepen your understanding of the rules and principles that apply.

It is important to see through the illusions. The astral spheres are full of illusions. But alleged "spiritual truths" can also turn out to be false.

Analysing things carefully and leaving illusions behind will increase our freedom. The freedom to dive into the various universes, as well as the freedom to exit them at any time.

This freedom is the condition for the following telepathic work with unfree beings.

Find out if the following instructions are useful to you. - If not, I can offer my assistance and help you.

My reservation:

I do not work with magic. It is not my goal to fight and to defeat others. I will not give my assistance if revenge, punishment or oppression is envisaged.

Each and every being has the same right to be here and/or to become free. I follow strict spiritual-ethical rules and offer the knowledge that can liberate.

Telepathic Liberation Procedure, Step-by-Step

When I encounter beings, I do not search for designations or names. As soon as I know on which level a being is and/or what intentions and aims he/she has, I can start with my work.

- And, as in other cases, also here it applies: I do not work over someone's head. It is not helpful nor is it ethical to liberate someone from occupation by foreign beings without the person's consent. It would be an intrusion that just causes bewilderment and confusion.

- When I do work for myself, it is up to me to define on which level the being - or group of beings - is. Sometimes it is absolutely clear, even in my day-time awareness. If not, my Higher Self will know it as soon as contact has been established.

- The level defines how powerful the beings are. Once more, an overview:

- On level 7 we will meet, for example, disoriented deceased persons who have not noticed that they are dead or those who believed that everything would be over after death. They generally think in materialistic terms and are scared to lose the life they have already lost.

  These beings often attach themselves to our lower chakras and may be the cause of sudden pain in the lower parts of our body or in the legs and feet. These beings are in great fear. We become aware of their presence because we ourselves are all of a sudden fearful without any reason.

- On level 8 we will meet those beings who mainly define themselves through emotions. They feel lonely and abandoned, they long for security, and they need acknowledgement and appreciation. Most probably, such beings have had previous incarnations in which they were devalued or ignored.
  Such beings now look for humans with the emotional quality that seems to offer exactly what they are longing for.
  Such foreign occupations are not easily identified. However, when we feel strangely burdened or even depressive, in spite of our nature and without any reason, it is important to ask the relevant questions.

  On level 8 we will also meet those beings with sexual

intentions. Here also it applies: if our sexuality seems to take on a life of its own, it is advisable to search – also in the astral realms - for the source of influence.

Many an "angel" or alleged "Jesus" will talk to us from level 8 and should be liberated.

- On level 9 are those who want power. The weaker ones among them follow the orders of a "commander". They have themselves been devaluated and are programmed in a certain sense. These beings seem to us to be very powerful, but they are not really. However, we only realize that the moment we have enough power to look them in the eye.

We do have the possibility to grow step by step and to improve our communication skills. Whoever accepts this challenge will eventually meet the most powerful ones, the self-proclaimed gods, who are at the top of the hierarchy.

Humans have given them many names: the Devil, Daemons, Anunnaki, Reptilians, Archons … But it is also the Archangels – and often a pretended "Jesus" turns out to be a level 9 being.

The "Jesus"-disguise is also used by beings on levels 7 and 8. This disguise is very successful and therefore popular. Well, yes, I know that sounds like blasphemy. But I cannot sufficiently caution about the great astral masquerade!

The rulers of level 9 will immediately make the hierarchy clear and will place themselves above you. Or they will ignore you if they feel you are not important enough.

Now it will depend on you, on whether you can make it clear to them that you are equal. We have to defy them! There is no place for fear here. As soon as you can brave their presence and look at them eyeball to eyeball, they will respect you.

And now – only now – you show them that you are capable of rising above the astral realms. You present yourself as you are while in meditation, for example in the loving quality of level 10.

We will be capable of doing all of the above, if we have experienced all the spiritual universes during meditation and if we are – through regular practice – in a good contact with the spiritual qualities of consciousness. During meditation we can experience our inviolability, and that will enable us to face the beings of level 9 without any fear.

If you are authentic and credible, they will respect you, even bow to you and then go away. But you will not be able to bluff them!

Once I have determined on which level the being – or group of beings – is, I find out what his/her/their intention is:

a) **Needs help**
It is possible that a being, or a group of beings, is distressed and desperate and is looking for help.
The contact with desperate beings full of fear is no less unpleasant than the attack of an angry being. The contact to fearful beings can often cause palpitations of the heart, headaches, a burning sensation in the bladder, diarrhoea ... However, what seemed dark and evil at the beginning may often, when looking more closely, just be desperation.

b) **"Evil"**
It can be that the being wants to defeat me or even destroy me. There can be many reasons for this. The reasons may be valid or not:

- the being feels disturbed by my actions
- perhaps I did not respect his alleged territory
- the being wants to take revenge for a past event
- the being feels good when it can dominate me
- the being wants to prevent me from becoming/being free
- the being is following orders

We can only communicate efficiently and solve the situation once we know the issue.

Let's first Deal with those Looking for Help

In such cases we often have to do with deceased people. Sometimes we meet individual beings, sometimes they come in groups. All of them have gone through horrible experiences. They may have been refugees, boat people, victims of war, torture, exploitation, catastrophes, accidents or diseases.

They all had plans for their lives and now feel duped and cheated, without a future. They often complain about the injustices they experienced and do not know how to continue.

Sometimes, there are beings who never incarnated on Planet Earth. They had their horrible adventures in the astral universes, where the experiences are generally much more unsettling than on Earth. These beings also have been made to forget who they really are.

What we Can Do to Liberate those Needing Help

We listen to them attentively and with an open heart, giving their pain a space in our compassion. We respect the beings, take their pain seriously, and we apologize in the name of those who were unjust to them.

The more sincere we are in our sympathy, the easier it is for the beings to let go of their pain.

Once the emotions have subsided, we let them know that there is an end to pain; that as spiritual beings they can be completely free of pain and that we will show them who they really are.

At this precise moment, I show myself as a free, bright being, just as I experience myself during meditation.

I put my whole spiritual knowledge at their disposal. The beings are thus reminded of their own knowledge.

Afterwards, together we go back in time up to the point where these beings also experienced themselves as free spiritual beings, because "those who remember gain consciousness" (title of my first book).

What we Need to Know in Order to Handle "Evil"

"Evil" beings know all of our weak points and they also know all the tricks to credibly demonstrate their reign of terror. We will only be able to defy them with sufficient knowledge and with a powerful energetic presence. The "evil" beings will lie to us. It is up to us to unmask those lies.

The following statements are often made by "evil" beings:

— **"You belong to me and I dominate you."**

> To know that we only belong to ourselves and that no one has the right to dominate us in the spiritual realm will give us power. This lie will be easily vetoed.

— **"You have sinned and I am here to punish you."**

> Those who have already cleared karma will reply self-

confidently: "Let my sins be my business. I take full responsibility for my karma. You do not have the right to punish me."

— **"I am GOD and I decide what is to happen here."**

Your answer will be: "I know that I am a divine being. A being who wishes to rule and to dominate like you do is far away from divinity. Don't bother me."

— **"I will destroy you, I have the power to do so."**

Your answer: "I know that you can destroy my body. But that will be of no use to you because I am a free immortal being."

— **"You have interfered in my game and I will now punish you for that."**

It may be that this being is angry because we freed a being who was being oppressed by him. If we did an ethically clean job, we can reply with a good conscience:
"That being wanted to become free, so I offered him my knowledge. You do not have the right to hold someone captive against his will."
"I have a right to be here and I also have a right to offer my knowledge. I respect free will and so will you, because we all have the right to self-determination."
"I will not destroy your game and I do not give you the right to destroy mine."

— **Sometimes it happens that the evil-looking being wants to become free.**

Naturally, he/she has the right to become free and we will show him/her the necessary steps.

Karma

Beings going through a regression and reaching the point in time where they are still in contact with their true spiritual nature, experience a state of being of deep knowledge and all-embracing love. This enables them to clear their whole karma and to dissolve or "undo" everything they created. That is necessary in order to be completely free. Even those beings acting destructively "solely" as a consequence of programming are responsible for their acts.

By cheating, oppressing, manipulating or acting destructively we constantly increase the number of our enemies. Sooner or later, these will return to us with their whole pain and anger. And that is a good thing!

In such a way we will be able to realize that we have barred a part of creation (human beings, but also animals or plants) from our love and responsibility. These excluded beings will in turn push destructively into our reality until we take back responsibility and reconcile.

The law of cause and effect is a physical one. The effect is unavoidable and the law has no expiry date. The energy we set in motion will come back to us. From a spiritual point of view, we are everything. So, whatever we cut-off from us will roll back to us. That is the only way we will be able to attain perfection, wholeness.

These rules apply to all: astral beings, deceased ones, human beings, you and me. These rules have not been defined or created by anyone. They are simply consistent, just as any physical law.

The more spiritual work we do with other beings, the better we will understand this logic.

We can dissolve our karma in a very efficient manner once we have walked the path right to the end, once we have experienced the Numinous and have recognized our own divinity. From then on, it will be absolutely natural to meet every being (victim or perpetrator) with empathy. We will listen to them sympathetically, we will apologize for the pain they have gone through, we will forgive them and we will remind them of their own innate spirituality.

So, we can become free, even before we die.

The Spiritual Realms

If you work in an operating theatre, you learn to accurately differentiate between "inside" and "outside" the theatre. Inside there are strict rules to be followed in order to ensure sterile conditions. It is a world of its own.

Similarly, the spiritual universes are separated from the worldly stage (physical world) and from the control room (astral realms). In numerous aspects the spiritual universes are **the exact opposite** of the other worlds.

Many years ago, a text by Rudolf Steiner captured my attention. In his book on evil (original Title "Mysterium des Bösen"), Rudolf Steiner writes that humans can hardly cope with evil unless they come to an understanding of why evil needs to be in this world. That understanding is then reached when we realize that evil in the physical world is only **misplaced**. The same characteristics or properties that humans unjustly apply, thereby creating evil in the physical world, would result in advancement in the spiritual realms.

In my book "Gestrandete Engel" (meaning "Stranded Angels", print edition coming soon), I write about this so-called "being misplaced" described by Rudolf Steiner, i.e. the irreconcilability and dichotomy of Heaven and Earth. This publication was meant to reassure and to give orientation to those spiritual beings who had decided to incarnate here on Earth, in order to participate in the game of creation, but who had not yet fully understood that other rules apply here.

Many of those beings cracked or have devaluated themselves, believing they were not normal … To those stranded angels I want to give a hand and try to ease their situation.

However, not only is it difficult to live here on Earth as a spiritual being, it is particularly difficult to return to those spheres where everything is so different.

The eye of the needle is extremely small.

The threshold to the spiritual realms is the most heavily guarded border in the whole universe.

Only those capable of letting go of all their attachments – at least temporarily – and whose longing and love for the spiritual source are strong enough will be let through the eye of the needle – at least temporarily – in order to reach the spiritual qualities.

In other words: by letting go of our attachments, we refine the frequency of our consciousness until we find ourselves in another universe – which, in fact, is in the same place, but has another vibrational frequency.

Trying to name and understand new experiences – even in meditation – using the familiar tools of the left-side brain, will prevent the refining of consciousness frequency and therefore hamper the attainment of spiritual qualities. For the rational type human being it is very difficult to do without these familiar and intimate tools.

> *That is possibly also the reason why many take drugs, in order to switch off rational thinking. – Although I know that a few serious seekers could actually open a door to new insights using drugs, I would never recommend drugs. Too many have landed with drugs in an illusionary world that has absolutely nothing to do with spirituality.*

Mental processes, questioning, researching, reflecting and understanding are an important and valuable preparation for meditation. When the mind understands, it quiets down. Secrets keep the mind active. The mind wants solutions, it needs to understand.

Being forced to believe something unexplainable, just because it is a dogma, is a form of mind control. Our awareness is corrupted and confused when we are forced to consider "wonders" and illogical things as truths.

Believing means not knowing; i.e. the issue has not been experienced or understood. This kind of blind belief is in my view destructive.

Personal experiences are different. They give us certainty. The risk of misinterpreting the experience remains high enough. However, the misinterpretation will become evident at some point.

Left-side brain thinking is obstructive for meditation. It is much better to listen to your senses and feelings. I am talking about an all-embracing, subtle awareness, about a silent presence.

As long as we hear words during meditation, as long as verbal language exists, we find ourselves in the astral realms. Language is inexistent in the spiritual spheres.

The Function of the Higher Self

I call the levels 10, 11 and 12 the Higher Self.

> During meditation, we actually **become** level 10, level 11 or level 12 beings, i.e. without a physical body, like an angel. We become one with the corresponding quality.
>
> The immediate consequence: we can no longer judge. The question is no longer: good or evil. Instead, we recognize whether something corresponds to the spiritual truth or is far from it.
>
> Addressing one's Higher Self directly from day-time awareness feels different. We remain who we are, man or woman. We look up at the Higher Self in order to obtain orientation.
>
> The Higher Self, similar to a guardian angel, helps to take a decision. Caution: the Higher Self does not answer verbally. But you will feel which option gives you more energy.

During meditation, it is advisable to focus on a specific spiritual quality, e.g. compassion. To contemplate, to approach and to touch it until, with time, we become one with this quality.

It is like looking at something yellow for a long time, until we feel that we have ourselves become thoroughly yellow.

We get into the flow, feeling compassion or gratefulness, or any other aspect we wish to experience, and after a while we feel we have become compassion or gratefulness. That may take some time, depending on how far we have drifted away from that quality.

The Qualities of the Three Spiritual Levels

- Level 10 stands for love, compassion and mercy towards the whole of creation, towards the limitless universe.
- Level 11 stands for a light-hearted, joyful quality expressed in ethereal sounds, colours and shapes. Everything is an endless happy dance.
- Level 12 is a state of all-embracing knowledge. Nothing remains hidden. We experience that nothing is separate from us. We can interpenetrate everything and therefore understand everything. There is no impulse for action, because "it is as it is and everything may be as it is".

This might sound like idle talk for someone who does not meditate and who has not experienced this spiritual consciousness. I often witness that even an astral being is addressed as "Higher Self" who, enjoying his power, gives an answer.

Sometimes, it is also a part of one's own ego that is used in order to legitimate certain actions.

That is just about as spiritual as footballers kissing the ground before the game starts.

The Border Is Well Guarded

I cannot repeat it often enough: the boundary between the astral regions and the spiritual realms is the most heavily guarded border in the whole universe. The beings are held back with all sorts of tricks.

Religious movements are started and after a short while they are corrupted. What starts with good intentions is infiltrated by astral powers blocking the way to freedom. Indeed, liberation is not a group movement, characterised by same clothing, same songs and, especially, not manifested in the feeling of exclusively knowing the right path. Liberation is to be found in the resoluteness of autonomous individual beings, although one will of course help friends.

Alertness is of utmost importance.

A spiritual path is very personal, individual and no two paths are similar.

On such a holistic healing path many injuries, blockades and dogmas need to be healed and cleared away. That is the only way to understand and to realize divine consciousness.

Neither the performance of rituals nor the strict following of instructions will lead to success, because there is no one "up there" who will praise and say "well done!" Were it so, we would not be free spiritual beings, but merely children.

On the spiritual path we are driven by an active interest. We long for knowledge and are not satisfied by superficial answers. We are prepared to make sacrifices. In the end, it is all about finding our inner divinity.

In the meantime, the majority of our fellow human beings will be following the instructions that have been programmed for slaves: to earn enough financial and other means, in order to satisfy their never ending superficial needs.

It is good to know that in all religions and in all peoples, there have been and still are individual beings who have recognized and accomplished true spirituality and who know the way out.

Those who have walked the path stand as examples for mankind and, as such, incarnate the most precious. They are generally not interested in being in the limelight. True seekers will recognize them.

The problem is there are hardly any true seekers these days.

The majority would prefer to take the sweet sugar pills of enlightenment ...

To seek? To work for it?

Perhaps for years? Even every day?

To regularly take time to sit down – not in front of TV, but in quiet meditation?

The System has done a very good job to keep us away from it, hasn't it?

Those who have made it their priority to research in the field of consciousness and who are prepared to walk the path have become rare.

Our life has become very demanding. Any possible inspiration is helpful. I also like to be inspired by books and speeches (YouTube is full of them). I enjoy inquisitive minds and every crumble of truth. They give me the joyful feeling that there are companions on the path.

> You are holding this book in hands.
> There is a reason for it ...
> Most probably you are no longer a beginner!
> My congratulations! You made it up to here.
> The most difficult part is already behind us.

Perhaps you have already taken the categorical decision and, by doing so, you have felt that your consciousness frequency immediately changed when you said to yourself something like:

"Yes, I want to walk the path. Yes, my consciousness is very important to me. I want to do research on the subject of consciousness and I want to experience enlightenment."

If the signal is clear, and it is not just an elusive thought, help will be there. That is how the spiritual laws work.

Compassion and All-Embracing Love on Level 10

The best way to take a break from our 3D-world fully consciously is certainly to go within and, in quiet contemplation, contact the spiritual qualities.

- It might be easier to dissolve the identification with the body and with the worldly role after some careful work involving bodily, emotional and energetic matters.
- We wake up in the consciousness frequency of level 10 and experience that we ourselves actually are those all-loving, compassionate beings!
- Enjoy the nectar of spiritual love.
- It may become evident that this love is the most powerful thing there is because it makes us inviolable and invincible. We are immortal.
  Our physical body remains vulnerable, of course. Just as our emotional body too. Consisting of subtle matter, it can be injured or taken hold of. The spiritual being has no mass and therefore nothing and nobody can stand in its way.
- Dwelling here on level 10 means that all personal injuries and all intentions have been left behind. Enjoy the closeness of level 10 beings. They are good guides and there is much to learn.
- Our love will grow and become all-embracing until we feel the same love towards every existing being.
  That does not mean that we agree with the actions of egos. The goal is to see through all layers of devaluations, programming, as well as through all karmic issues, until we reconnect with the divine core.

We love the being, not the ego. We just acknowledge the presence of the ego.

And no, I am not saying this happens in life. This happens in meditation.

We have to find a way to leave personal issues behind us, in order to access an objective reference point. We know that:

Problems cannot be solved at the same level they were created. And we cannot solve them with the same consciousness level that created the problems.

On level 10 we are beyond the stage. We look at the things happening, but not with the eyes of the stage director, giving instructions from just across. Our spiritual hands rest in our lap. We are like angels, sitting on a cloud, attentively observing the course of events, without interfering.

We rise above and beyond the problems and we re-tune our "instrument", our awareness, our consciousness. In the spiritual condition of being, there is no emotional staining. There are no egotistical wishes or longings. The I, every ME and MINE, are silent and calm. We are objective and clear.

We see the big picture, a picture not limited by birth and death. We can allow every being to make its own choices. We do no longer join sides, taking the one against the other side. Now the bigger connections become visible.

In this re-tuned state, after meditation, we will find wise(r) solutions to our problems and challenges.

Comparing Levels 4 and 10

The difference between levels 4 and 10 lies in the personal love compared to the non-personal, all-embracing spiritual love.

As already mentioned, we all have partially broken hearts. That is part of human life. That can be, and should be, an incentive for inner work, because with an injured heart we impart injuries. We can only give what we have.

Therefore, we will nurture our heart and cultivate our compassion.

This work will lead us to a difficult lesson:

The time will come when the world becomes unbearable. There is just too much injustice and too much suffering.

At this time there is a real danger of becoming angry and letting our Solar Plexus (level 3) take the lead. We want to fight and end the misery.

Or we switch on our throat-chakra (level 5), write pamphlets and issue calls to resistance.

All of these inputs are valuable. Change always follows discontentment. Moreover, changes are of great importance because they induce new growth.

However, your heart will be no less painful! We will only find salvation on level 10.

I know that the fighters among us will not like this statement. They will talk of escapism ...

Both realities collide just here. There will never be a conciliation or settlement.

A different logic applies in the spiritual realms. From the spiritual point of view, the game on Earth is a condensed illu-

sion.
It is certainly possible to shift energies around in this game, but the dynamics will not change. One thousand, two or even three thousand years ago there was proportionally no less suffering and misery.

Decide for yourself which way you want to take:

Do you want to use your power to change the world?

Or do you want to walk a spiritual path?
(It could be that things do change as a consequence of your spiritual path. Not as a consequence of your actions, but as a consequence of your being.)

And the next question:

In how many lives have you already tried to change the world?

From a spiritual point of view, the solution lies in quitting that level of frequency, to realize enlightenment, in order to come back. As a "lighthouse" we can give orientation, and we can reach a hand to those who also want to become free.

There Is quite a Bit to Say about Compassion

Compassion is one of the really important spiritual qualities. Compassion makes us soft, tender and invincible at the same time.

It is extremely painful to meet the big "wrongdoers" of this world with compassion. After all, they have caused quite a bit of suffering.

Spiritual compassion is based on the understanding that in the end we are all one and that each and every single being comes from the same Source.

Therefore, there is really only one possibility to improve the situation:

It is about meeting these beings (not their egos), standing next to them, reviewing with them everything they have done, but also everything they have had to endure until they became the perpetrators. What was done to them was also done to us.

In such a way we begin to understand, to forgive and to ask for forgiveness.

The pain these beings have had to endure often moved me to tears.

Many perpetrators are looked upon as "the Evil in person". They carry the whole hate of the masses on their shoulders.

Today I can appreciate and value the chance we have in meeting these "perpetrators-victims" and unwaveringly addressing ourselves to their innate inner light. It is like striking a bell that has not rung for decades, centuries, perhaps even eons.

Yes, these beings can be freed and rehabilitated. And it is overwhelming to see that such powerfully destructive beings can represent spiritual qualities just as powerfully, once they have recovered their resplendence and their love.

Every single being, no matter if black, red, yellow, brown or white, no matter if humanoid, reptoid, insectoid, aquatic, good or evil, comes from the Numinous, originates from the same Source.

Beings are beings. They all belong in this endless universe.

Our ability to accept all and to concede the right of existence to all is the measure of our love.

That has nothing to do with the fact that we as humans have to and need to set limits, over and over again.

And what Exactly Is Spiritual Healing?

Spiritual Healing exists, no question about that.

Spiritual Healing has to do with *becoming whole*. Physical healing is not the main issue here.

We come closer to *being whole* when all our aspects – body, emotions, mind and spirituality – are awakened and increasingly reconciled.

By doing so, blockages, dogmas, ego intentions and negative emotions are dropped out and the organising spiritual principle is activated. Even if bacteria, viruses or injuries by accident are involved, this organising principle will also be positively effective.

(If the causes for the disease are to be found in the astral realm, the organising principle will bring us in a clear state of mind/consciousness, allowing us to confront these influences.)

Very often, the healing is triggered by the encounter with an awakened person. The encounter can be on the physical or on the spiritual plane. The goal is the willingness to let the spiritual organising principle take the lead.

It is a sweeping change. You will not be the same after such an experience.

Naturally, such a change can also occur without a previous disease. The reason why this is seldom the case, is to be found in the willpower of human beings. We want to get better, but we also want to continue living as before. This sort of whole spiritual healing is not possible if the attachments and intentions contradict the spiritual essence.

Interference and Influence Disempower Us

The difference between external influence and real spiritual assistance is important and decisive.

There is for example the mother, standing next to the child at the edge of the swimming pool, saying with insistence and best intentions:
"Pluck up your courage, you can do it, I count on you, I trust you, don't be a quitter, you can really do it ..."

Friends believe they can help when they powerfully give advice: *"You have to quit this job, you have to leave this partner, that is making you sick. I have already told you many times that ... Why don't you listen to me?"*

And healers suggest: *"Just believe it. Visualise it in all detail in your mind and the healing has already taken place ..."*

Visualisation and visions are not basically wrong. What is negative here is the power that the healer pumps into the process: do this; do that; trust me; I know it (better than you) ..." The world is full of them.

With powerful intention, and always in the belief of doing a favour to the other, "love" or "energy" is forced onto the other person. The following example is possibly the worst case:

> *A client of mine told me: "Every single day I send love to my boss."*
> *I: "Oh, really? Do you love your boss?"*
> *Client: "No, I hate him!"*
> *I: "And where do you get the love from?"*
> *Client: "It is cosmic love."*
>
> *Cosmic love? An absolute fantasy, having nothing to do with spiritual truth.*
> *I imagine the "love gift" left the boss somewhat confused.*

"Helpers' " Help

There are three possible ways.

Thesis: *The well-meant advice from the "helper" is not followed.*

The "victim" carries on complaining about the unsatisfactory partnership, about the unfavourable working conditions, etc.

Frustration grows in the "helper". *"I give my very best. But he/she just does not want to listen!"* Gradually rejection increases, perhaps even condemnation, and the relationship might break up.

Anti-Thesis: *The "victim" follows the advice given.*

The "helper" has the satisfaction that now something is changing and that the time invested seems to have been worthwhile.

The "helper" will soon find out that, in the eyes of the "victim", he/she is also responsible for the consequences of the changes.

Synthesis: *The "helper" assists the "victim" in the decision-making process.*

The child at the swimming pool would be asked: *"What would you need to be able to jump into the water?"*

The child might want to first jump in a few times where the water is not so deep … In such a way the child takes its own decision and learns to better perceive its own needs. The child choses to make an experience and is thereby not left alone.

Or one could tell about one's own experience: *"When I was a child, it was helpful to count to three and then jump. The most important was that I was convinced of my decision. Then I could actually jump."* The child will then decide for itself if this method can be adapted to its own needs. This kind of assistance might turn into a lesson for life.

The friend with the unsatisfactory partnership will be asked: *"What do you like about this partnership? Where would you like to be with this relationship in a year's time? What could you do to achieve that goal? Does your partner also want that? Is the goal realistic? Can you think of a possible alternative? How can I help you?"*

In such a way this friend stays in his/her situation and in his/her own power.

"Victims' " Behaviour

Thesis: *The "victim" is given advice.*
The advice increases the inner tenseness and intensifies the feeling of not being capable. The energy decreases.

Anti-Thesis: *The "victim" behaves as told.*
The "victim" is not "in his/her own strength", relying instead on the advisors. The "victim" has absorbed the willpower of the advisors or obeys – remaining childish. *"I do it because I trust you."*

If the result is positive, it may somehow be acceptable. If the result is negative, blaming logically threatens. In any case, dependency rather than freedom is created.

Synthesis: *The "victim" decides on the steps to be taken at his/her own speed.*
The "victim" has decided to change some things. The assistance of the "helper(s)" increases courage and clarity, allowing enough room for the "victim" to take the decisions that feel right to him/her. The "victim" retains the responsibility and acts out of its own strength.

The learning process takes place by walking the path step by step. The journey is the reward …

We are in this world in order to experience things. And we all have the right to make these experiences at our own speed.

The point is not to pump in energy into a given situation. The idea is to provide enough room, to point out the possible alternatives and to be present in a wise manner.

We can practice the correct attitude and communication when working with our own body cells. They have already known for long what their job is. It is often our tenseness and anxiety that makes life difficult for them. With more energy and intent we only increase the pressure. It is better to relieve and unburden, so that the cells can act freely. The same rules apply when dealing with human beings.

Healing in the spiritual sense is a holistic process and not an abracadabra miracle method that transforms a situation in its opposite. We can practice healing every day: with the body, with all the small injuries and aches, in the communication with our cells, as described above.

Treating every headache with a painkiller, *suppressing* every fever, immediately *killing* all bacteria with antibiotics and never learning to attend to your body during a healing process will automatically lead to requesting major intervention in case of more serious illness.

Happiness and Joyful Creativity on Level 11

We continue our meditative journey and open up to the upper octave of the fifth chakra.

- Focus your concentration in your Third Eye and relax.
- Do not rise above your body but try to dissolve the identification with your body, as if you would leave behind an old coat.
 There is no need to go anywhere. By changing the frequency of your consciousness, the endless space will open up.
 Be aware of the fact that you are a free spiritual being. Should you need to give yourself a form or shape, you can create one playfully within fragments of a second. The form does not need to have arms or legs.
- I wish you could see the joyful relief of those beings (e.g. dead ones we have helped to become free) who have learned to leave all the heaviness behind them.

While I write these lines, I naturally go into resonance with the subtle energies of level 11. We can meet there at any time! Each and every contact thrills my Higher Self (Level 10, 11 or 12)!

I would like to remind you of this absolute freedom, exempt of any fear. I would like to show you the pure joy, the laughter, the sounds, the light and the effortlessness of playful dances so that you can enjoy the multidimensional energy patterns.

Unfortunately, many do not come into contact with these amazing qualities because many layers of fear and anxiety lie in between. If you wish, I can give you a hand – metaphorically speaking. But only if you really want it. You are absolutely free to make your own decisions, at all times.

- After meditation, we return to our daily affairs. We "refill" our body with our presence, we once again take responsibility for our goods and chattels and go back to our tasks.

- By travelling between these worlds daily, it becomes evident that life on Earth is a temporary play. What matters in this play is not really earthly success. The experiences we make and the conclusions we draw from these experiences are much more important.

There Is No Hurting on Level 11

Painful experiences are part of human life on Earth. Would it not be so, we would probably become lethargic and decadent.

Loved ones die, friendships break up, all sorts of losses are experienced and the ageing process can be quite a challenge. To be aware of the physical decline of the body is not easy. We have to bow out of dreams and visions and we have to accept that younger ones take over the reins.

All of this belongs to a privileged life. Let us not forget the ones who really suffer!

Those who only know the worldly reality will have to work hard to maintain their laughter and the brightness in their eyes right up to old age.

Through regular spiritual meditation, the priorities are shifted. With time it becomes easier to let go – at least temporarily – of the worldly attachments. What caused fear at the beginning, becomes more and more a gasp of relief. As the identification with the spiritual freedom increases, the attachments decrease. That is good so!

We rehearse leaving everything behind us every day. The experience of being whole and perfect, of not needing anything, of not losing anyone becomes increasingly familiar. By doing so, our everyday lives will be influenced more and more.

In the spiritual realms we do not lose any friends, because we can always find them again and meet them spiritually at any time.

We can invite those who linger in denser spheres – during lifetime or after death – to revisit their immanent wholeness and to become free.

Should a being decide to remain and act in the denser spheres, it will be easier for us to accept it from the spiritual perspective than it would be to witness, as a human being, how someone succumbs to addiction or delinquency.

Everybody has the right to walk labyrinthine paths and to take new decisions at any time.

The beings we meet in level 11 are not interested in the physical and astral universes. Their undivided attention is set on the joyful self-expression and the play as such, where there is no suffering. Even the frequency of compassion is missing here on level 11, since there is no suffering that would call for compassion.

There is not the slightest trace of fear on level 11. It is absolutely clear that nobody could force us to do anything here.

I would like to repeat that astral beings have mass. Mass is created by aggregation, concretion, by ego intentions, attachments, emotions, etc. These are aspects we have already transcended here on level 11.

Every being who has experienced fear and horror can be captured and imprisoned. Though the prison is preconceived and illusionary, it will become compelling if the victim can be convinced of its existence.

Young elephants are tied to a pole with a rope during the night. They get used to waiting patiently for the mahout to come in the morning. The grown-up elephants would actually be strong enough to rip the rope. Nonetheless, they don't do it, because they do not question their captivity.

Spiritual beings see through the illusion. Those who know who they really are cannot be lied to and cannot be frightened.

There are no desires or longings on level 11 because we are immediately present there where we turn our attention to. We can also be everywhere simultaneously. Space-time is not compelling for free consciousness.

In contrast, astral trips or remote viewing take place in the astral realms, usually on level 7.

The awareness on level 11 is not focused on material things. Therefore, neither enemy weapon systems nor underground bunkers could be detected. Spiritual "seeing" is absolutely useless for military purposes – and that is the best protection.

Sometimes, the beings in level 11 show themselves in a certain shape. When they want someone to recognize them, they can create an image from a previous incarnation and, for example, make contact in a dream. This is possible from all spiritual realms (10, 11, 12). Generally, the shape is rather ethereal and has no mass at all.

Creative Expression on Level 11

Creativity belongs to our essence. We create from ourselves in a constant, joyful self-expression.

Beings are constantly emitting or beaming out sparks of consciousness. Just as all our body cells have the same genetic make-up, so are all our sparks of consciousness distinctive holographic images of our self. By beaming out these sparks of consciousness, we are multiplying ourselves, so to say. Generally, these sparks of consciousness are taken back after a while. They are de-created. Or, they are forgotten and remain in the game ...

Furthermore, qualities can be impressed onto these sparks of consciousness: colour, an energetic direction, expansion or contraction, angular momentum, and later on, after they have sunk into the denser universe, also emotions such as grief, pain, longing, anger.

Just as images on the screen are composed of pixels, so are the multi-dimensional happenings composed of sparks of consciousness; in fact, every concept, every shape, every colour, every sound, every atom ...

The beings on level 11 just love this endless diversity of forms and colours swaying playfully. The game always remains light and unburdened at all times.

Willpower is just as inexistent as goals to be reached are. And, as in all spiritual realms, no spoken language exists. There is just no need for it. Nothing needs to be explained; everything is plainly obvious.

The sparks of consciousness left back in the game gradually condense and build up the smallest parts of matter (Quarks). With time, these turn into atoms, molecules, molecule chains. That is the matter that makes up the creation game. In this way, we have all contributed to creation. We are still doing it right now and continue doing it every single day.

Just in case you would want to increase your freedom, it is advisable to call back your sparks of consciousness. It is just as if you would inhale what you once exhaled.

Unfortunately, it is difficult to describe these things more accurately. Therefore, I would like to invite you to try it out. If you have understood the principle, you will be able to do it.

And if you have spiritual awareness, you will be able to check if the procedure worked.

Nature is an Image of the Timeless Beauty of Level 11

Beauty, aesthetics, elegance, playfulness – we cannot and do not want to deprive ourselves of the fascination of level 11. Being reminded of this enchantment during our earthly life touches us deeply. It is the dance of snowflakes, their perfect form, a rainbow, the fascination of a waterfall, an intact flower meadow, an intact piece of nature.

Musicians, composers, artists often have a strong link to level 11 and constantly try anew to bring a piece of Heaven down to Earth.

There are of course also those artists who worship the ugly, who reproduce "Hell" and who want to shock. After reading all previous chapters, you probably know where they get their inspiration from.

Quite different are those who seek to inform or to wake up through artistic means. They manage to present even topics difficult to cope with in a superior quality work.

We carry these magnificent qualities within. It is most recommendable to give such qualities enough room. Have you already taken time for it today?

All Embracing Awareness on Level 12

We have now taken the steps together, one after the other, i.e. I described the journey through its different qualities and I hope that you could experience them. So, with every step, you have had the feeling of your consciousness becoming lighter and lighter, freer, expansive, all-embracing, quiet and whole. You are now slowly beginning to sense the meaning of perfection, of divinity.

Good examples are a must on this path. Encounters, if possible with a living example, or at least spiritual encounters, remind us of the different qualities of consciousness. It is so easy to forget in our everyday life full or noise, smoke, luxury, superficialities, egoism.

A truthful encounter, at a time when we are really ready for it, spiritual being to spiritual being, will change our life. Qualities that have perhaps been buried deep down will be awakened – no bigger gift can be given to us.

"Divine Consciousness" is something REALLY big – and yet so simple.

It can take a long time before we allow this opening of consciousness. And then, when it happens, we will realize how affected and handicapped we have been by experiences made in our physical body.

> *Some time ago a group of seamen entered my awareness. They were shipwrecked about 200 years ago and were still caught in a time-bubble. They felt abandoned and needed help. I asked the group's spokesman: "What were you before being a seaman?" His answer: "Also a seaman." "And before that?" He had no other vision than to be a seaman and to navigate on all oceans. – It took a long time before he could be reminded of his spiritual existence with all-embracing consciousness.*

Forgetting soon becomes oblivion. And oblivion sweeps over everything at a speed we would not imagine possible.

Just as many deceased ones, the seamen depended on another person to communicate with them and to show them what it means to be spiritually free. Otherwise they would have remained in their bubble.

By the way, the seamen were on level 7, i.e. very close to physical reality.

If you only remember previous lives as a woman, you will no longer be able to remember how it feels to be a man. Culture, race and social stratum also leave their traces and inhibit our imagination.

"Spiritual" experiences are often described to me as if they would follow a material logic. It becomes clear that the jump into the spiritual dimensions has not yet taken place. As already described, divine consciousness is all-embracing and has nothing to do with the consistency of linear, physical logic. Everything is possible and may be. Everything is part of the whole and nothing is excluded. The awareness is interdimensional.

On level 10, love is so all-embracing that all beings are as close as brothers and sisters.

On level 12 the boundaries are dissolved and we see other beings as if they were part of ourselves. Our consciousness pervades everything in equal measure.

Nonetheless, there is still individuality. We are aware of a faint feeling of "I". An "I" without any trace of vanity or arrogance; an "I" with a deep understanding of everything that is.

On Level 12 We Are Whole and Autonomous

The question about belonging does not arise here. On level 12 we are simultaneously the drop and the ocean. There is nothing at all we would need from others because our innermost is the Numinous – and that is perfection, divinity.

On level 12 we are everything

Everything that exists is an expression of the highest essence. This quality is often called Om, sacred sound, source of everything. Some define love or light as the source of everything.

Love, light, sound: they are all similarly adequate descriptions of something that is beyond our earthly logic.

Most importantly: We carry this quality within

No being is superior. No being is inferior.
(Hierarchies belong to levels 1 to 9)

This is cause for great humbleness as well as for great dignity. We are divine beings amongst divine beings.

Ethics are experienced as an inner quality.

Enmity arises in denser spheres and presupposes a feeling of being separate.

Karma is fully understandable here.
It is like physics, an energetic dynamic force.

The logic of it is comprehensible:

Where there is an empty space, it gets filled.
Overweight tilts over into balance.
Resistance creates friction.
Whatever we exclude is forced upon us.
If you only fill one scale pan, life will fill the other one for you.

It is the game of forces – all in pursuit of balance.
Karma unfolds very naturally, all by itself.

Karma, i.e. attachments, can be dissolved. Love and knowledge are needed to do it ... You now know the principles. All great masters have spoken of it: it lies in our hands.

There is no anonymous god, whimsically administering rewards or punishments at his own discretion. By now, that should have become very clear.

It is our task to establish order. The easiest way to do it is with introspective spiritual work. It is not worthwhile to reincarnate in order to mend something because by the time we fix one thing, ten new attachments have developed.

No spiritual being will ever take on the role of an avenging angel. That is not its mission and is furthermore absolutely unnecessary. Those who distance themselves from spiritual love, deciding to play the role of the "bad guy", will pay the price by experiencing what it means to be cut off from spiritual love. – That's how easy it is.

Unbearable. Pure agony.

In our world there is Justice. It could be society's tool to guarantee fairness and to protect the people. Unfortunately, it often does not match our feeling of equitableness. This Justice has been created with the sole purpose of organizing the ownership of assets and human capital, so that the rulers can make their profits easily.

From a spiritual point of view, the point is just consistency. Consistency is straight forward, clear, incorruptible.

We are Brahma – Vishnu – Shiva.

We are the divine beings. We have the ability to create (Brahma), to sustain (Vishnu) and to dissolve (Shiva).

On level 12 we reach spiritual maturity. That implies great responsibility for the whole.

Responsibility? An unpopular concept in our ego-driven society where many understand spirituality to be like wellness, just much better! - And, of course, free of charge.

But spiritual maturity is about being present for others. Beings, as those seamen described above, need assistance and succour. Those who have completed the journey can offer spiritual succour.

We rest in being. Beeingness will cause change.

Let's Summarize

The challenges of life elicit very different reactions. At best, we will welcome the opportunity to test our abilities and tackle the problems at hand, like a good sport.

If you are not quite as fit, you will react with fear, insecurity, confusion and resentment. You may even be defiant and refuse to bow to the situation. If the challenge is such that we believe we are incapable of handling the situation, it might even cause disease.

Therefore, each challenge may cause us

- to fail and crash

- to stagnate, to run one's head against a brick wall, to persist defiantly

- to grow, become stronger and more capable

Spiritual work offers tools and techniques that make growth possible.

I have tried to provide an insight into the different themes. We all know, however, that a book cannot replace a therapeutic session.

Whether you do it on your own, or whether you have assistance, it is clear that a regular, if possible daily, clean-up (mental hygiene) is absolutely necessary.

Things become easier with time. The better we understand a certain subject, and the more thoroughly we have once cleared it up and healed it, the faster we will become aware of what is not in order.

The Steps Described so Far

- Take full possession of your personal chakras, sort out the corresponding themes and heal the chakras.

- Take your concentration to the Third Eye. Train and improve your ability to concentrate. The Third Eye is the portal to the spiritual realms.

- Withdraw from all worldly intentions.
  We just leave everything worldly behind us, take a break and enjoy the quieting down of our mind. The ability to leave the material world behind us, at least for a certain period of time, facilitates the spiritual meditation right up to the Source.

- After meditation we return to everyday life and take on responsibility. The break had an enormous positive effect on us.

- Very important: understand the rules of the astral realms. We have to experience all tools, techniques, mental states of the astral realms. We have to know what it is all about here. But first, we have to be securely anchored in the spiritual levels. Yes, it is quite possible that you first make sure you are settled in the spiritual levels before experiencing the astral worlds. The sequence - first astral worlds, then spiritual levels - is not compulsory.

Taking a Clear Decision Is Decisive

Those who enjoy getting into the act in the astral worlds have an energy that is too dense for the spiritual realms and will therefore not have access to them.

It is really a matter of taking a clear decision:

Astral or spiritual? Both at the same time are not possible. We are either in the pool and get wet, or we are outside of the pool, in the sun, and remain dry. But we cannot be in the pool and remain dry at the same time.

That means:

- Those who have their pipe dreams on level 7 (i.e. believing something will come through if only the dreams are precise and strong enough) will not be able to overcome these attachments.

- Those who seek emotional closeness to other beings on level 8 or who are regularly involved in sexual activities in the astral realms are too dense to experience spiritual qualities.

- Those who have a need for power and wish to control, and who act out these needs telepathically through the astral realms (erroneously believing no one notices), have similarly a dense frequency which will not permit access to more subtle realms.

But then, you might just want to experience those astral activities described above because you find them fascinating and exciting or because they give you a sense of superiority.

You have a right to it. – After all, this creation is here for the purpose of making experiences.

Everything has a right to exist. But there are things that are mutually exclusive. Every being must make its own choice. Some are magically attracted by the astral techniques, others have no interest whatsoever in them.

"Liberation" is the word on my banner. Liberation is not attainable in the astral realms. But you are free to take the side road to magical, suggestive, manipulative and shamanistic themes and I (temporarily) take my leave from you here.

My next steps lead to the spiritual qualities.

We all carry these qualities deep within, but they are easily overridden and forgotten.

We are Love and Compassion – Level 10
We are Joy and Lightness – Level 11
We are Everything and Everybody – Level 12

Of course, most of us need a bit longer to fully remember. It is a huge universe, but the principles are actually simple and logical.

Having come so far, we now have the Potential to accomplish our true divine nature

I have chosen these words intentionally: we really only have the *potential*. While meditating, many keep not only their eyes closed but also their perception.

"Enlightenment" does not fall into our lap just because we have followed the rules for long enough. Much more is needed, e.g. alertness, exploratory spirit, dedication, clever questioning, and courage! A lot of courage.

Open your inner eyes! Be alert and be open for this experience.

Meditation can be a fantastic voyage.

There is much to "explore". You have here the possibility to reach a profound understanding of whatever you want to know.

Where does evil come from? – Here you can comprehend.

Who am I really? – It will be revealed to you.

What is the purpose of this creation game? – You can explore the deeper meaning and you will find it.

It is a fantastic experience to find out that we can uncover all secrets and pierce all veils. At last there is peace.

Bliss on Level 13

The greater our longing to go home and the more familiar the subtle essence has become to us, the closer we'll nestle to spiritually and the easier it will be to merge.

At this point, I should stop talking, because everything I say will cause misunderstandings.

Nonetheless, I will try to describe, because keeping it secret will also be misunderstood.

> *It happens all of a sudden, unprepared, takes us in neck and crop, like a vortex, we are sucked in ...*
>
> *Everything expands in unbelievable love. We swim in a heaving ocean of love that encompasses us completely within and without ...*
>
> *Some say heaven has been torn open.*
>
> *Others describe hearing the hum of angels' fanfares.*
>
> *Still others perceive being pervaded by an unbelievable light that also pervades the whole universe.*

So much for the various trials to describe something unfathomable.

But, should anyone just wait to see the heaven tearing open, to hear the fanfares playing, the whole universe being pervaded by light and being overwhelmed by a wave of bliss, he/she will experience nothing of the sort.

I seldom speak of mercy. For level 13, I do.

What happens at this level cannot be provoked or controlled by us. If we just peacefully rest in love and enjoy being "at home", it may happen that, fully unexpectedly, we are embraced by a surge of bliss.

At the beginning, we will only be able to stay at this high quality level of consciousness for a short while. But, although of short duration, this experience will accompany and nurture us for years.

Coming Home

All reasons are good reasons to come home in the most subtle conscious quality of our being ...

Be it because we are endlessly happy, thankful and full of love. Or be it because we are endlessly suffering, are hopeless and have lost all orientation.

What happens here on Earth can sometimes be downright unbearable.

What used to be a playground has been turned into a battlefield.

The moves of the powerful are destructive, albeit inscrutable for many of us.

We see all the wounded hearts, we have compassion with all the exploited and oppressed ones, and we know that there is no end to it.

The longing to go home becomes compelling.

So, we take the time to pause.

The inner alignment brings peace.

Stress and resistance ease off. Emotions quiet down.

Thinking is no longer necessary because there is nothing flaring up requiring thought.

Quiet, at last.

These are merciful moments, when the mind becomes as placid as a mountain lake.

Not a single thought causes the surface of the water to be distorted.

The mountain lake becomes the perfect image of the sky. Not the slightest difference can be seen between above and below.

Endless perfection is imaged in our being in just this way.

It is the wonder of becoming one in the silence of meditation, as it is described by Indian mystics.

The Numinous

The Numinous – I chose this word for the highest spiritual quality of level 14, according to my chart in the chapter on Basic Information on the Chakras and Levels of Consciousness.

The Numinous is the origin, the Source of everything that exists. It is the all-embracing and all-pervading highest principle.

Time and time again I meet people who use the term "source" to designate something that communicates with us humans by way of language, telling us what to do and what not to do. However, a voice that gives instructions either comes from the astral realm or it is synthetic telepathy. That means, the voice is sent directly to the brain of human beings through modern technology. Such a voice never comes from the spiritual spheres!

A language comprises a limited number of words and these are moreover associated with different meanings. It is therefore of utmost importance to clearly define what we are talking about and what exactly we mean.

I hope that my explanations so far have made the differentiation of the various levels understandable.

The Numinous is the opposite of the whole diversity we see in all the universes, whether physical, astral or spiritual.

The Numinous is eternal, beyond time and space, it is not energy, it is formless and nameless.

The Numinous is not personified – and it never has intent.

The Numinous is solely potential. Everything can emerge from it.

The Numinous is unity. There is no subject who could observe an object. If you "die" in this Source, you will experience nothing, see nothing.

Whether you spend a second in the Numinous or whether you spend a million Earth years in it, it will feel the same. You are in timelessness. The surroundings, however, the complete game of creation, defined by matter, energy, time and space change constantly.

With a bit of practice, we can get used to diving into the Numinous while our body sleeps.

When waking up in the morning, it is valuable to spend a few minutes feeling the atmosphere experienced. Make sure all your cells can partake, all chakras are nourished and that your complete energy field is flushed with the experienced quality.

It is the sweet nectar of certainty that we have been in our true home.

We are a spark of consciousness – and, at the same time, we are also the whole.

The Master of the Key in Whitley Strieber's book "The Key" defines it as follows:

You are not only the crumb of a cake that can reunite with the cake. You can become the whole cake.

Strieber, Whitley. The Key: A True Encounter (Kindle-Position 697-701).

The mysterious visitor was asked: "Define ecstasy." Answer: "The energetic body has a spin, or vibration. This can go infinitely fast. It can reach beyond the speed of light, and exit time altogether. When this happens, the body begins to radiate of its own accord. It becomes at once God and co-creative with God, a companion. A single bit of God, which you are, does not only join the whole like a crumb in a cake, it can attain so much of ecstasy that it becomes the whole. Your destiny, each of you, is to become all of God."

When you wake up after visiting the Numinous, you will know your true nature. That is the resurrection of the spirit.

Go all the way right to the end and find out for yourself!

It Is Time for the Ultimate Step

With ultimate step I mean merging with the Numinous. We consciously allow the last tiny portion of ME to die. This step becomes possible when our love for the Highest is greater than our biggest fear:

The fear to disappear for ever – without a trace left.

This fear is just plain horror for many humans. It is the recurrent nightmare of falling into a deep black hole and disappearing for ever.

This might even be the reason for filling one's life with hundreds of distracting activities.

So, after going through all this spiritual work we land in a place that feels similar to before? – And we are supposed to confront just that same fear?

Exactly! – We are now powerful enough to do it.

Yes, unfortunately this scenario does not match the longings of the "Light-and-Love-Fraction". They would rather find themselves on an illusionary pink cloud, in endless bliss ...

Here we go: after all our experience in meditation we are ready.

We can allow ourselves to die,

to die in the Numinous.

We let go –

We become one where there are not two

and we lose consciousness ...

We allow ourselves to fall –

and we will not disappear forever –
but it feels so.

A paradox? For sure!

My First Conscious Dive

I had already been many years on my way, as one day during a still meditation, I unexpectedly realized that I could now let myself fall, and to dive into the Numinous. In ANAMI (the nameless).

My mind stepped in and I asked myself:

"Am I now ready to let it happen?"

I also checked:
-> are there any candles burning?
-> is the stove switched off?

And, although I expected this experience to end with death, I was absolutely sure: I had meditated all these years to experience exactly this.

I let myself fall – and I lost consciousness ...

After a while, I was here again – of course.

But now I knew who I am: ANAMI, nameless, eternal, divine consciousness.

Bliss!

The mystics say:

Those who give up everything, gain everything.

What now? What Is Different?

Is the drop that merged in the ocean still the same when it comes back?

Am I still me?

Yes, I am. In my purest essence.

The "drop" is a metaphor. It consists of numerous molecules with electrons, protons, neutrons and the tiny particles called quarks.

I, instead, as a spiritual being, am one. And as one I merge with the Numinous, in order to return enlightened as one.

It is exactly the same for you and for all existing beings.

Why is it important to dive into the Numinous if we do not see, do not hear, do not experience anything? What is the purpose of this experience?

Firstly: Only if our love is all-embracing and we are prepared to leave everything else behind can we merge with the Source. We can therefore check if we are deceiving ourselves.

Secondly: Only the Numinous is the complete Truth, everything else is an aspect of it, but not the whole. Just as the colours of the rainbow are aspects of the complete invisible light beam. The colours are recognizable *because* they are fragments.

After experiencing the Numinous, we will understand that we can only exist as beings because we are separate from the wholeness.

In the best of cases, we will represent truthfulness in an optimal way, never being able to represent it fully because we have separated ourselves from it in order to exist.

That will (hopefully) prevent us from becoming presumptuous, because our "I" is always second best.

I Have already Mentioned It

It is a narrow path leading to truthfulness.

Instead, the wide astral motorway with beautiful lanes (New Age and Esoterics, as often practiced today) is noisy and overpopulated. The goal here is to reach power, prestige and influence or an emotional well-being in the group. Every being takes decisions many times a day. Basically, the choice is between two priorities:

Priority physical world/astral realm or priority spirituality?

History has already repeated itself quite often. It would seem that all the innumerable beings would always want to repeat the same experiences ...

Spirituality is not a big thing and does not present itself as something spectacular or dramatic. It is just natural and stress-free. In spirituality we meet with humbleness, wisdom, dignity, love, compassion, understanding, patience, stillness ...

(However, I can become quite angry if someone expects me to support the life lies of his/her ego ...)

With a few beings we are spiritually closely linked. Perhaps we walk a part of the path together, sharing inspiring thoughts or just joyful stillness. These are relationships that remain unchanged, even beyond death.

It is wonderful if we can build up such a heavenly relationship with our closest ones. This is often prevented by the personal contact and we only realize what we have missed once we are "worlds" apart.

God

It is time now to look at the Divine Principle.

When speaking of "God", it is believed that we all have the same concept. However, that is seldom the case.

Who or what "God" means to us, whether that concept exists in our life or not, depends primarily on the upbringing and on the belief system in our environment. Especially in fundamentally religious cultures, religious allegiance is compulsory or even a matter of survival.

But, if the parents are moderate and the system allows religious freedom, even a child can start asking its own questions. Thus, tendencies that may have to do with experiences during previous incarnations or other lifeforms become visible. A child can be strongly drawn towards religious, spiritual themes, although the parents do not think much of such concepts. Or it can turn away from such subjects, although the parents are religious-minded.

What a great privilege it is to find out for oneself!

> *I was born into a moderate Protestant Christian home. As a child, I sent all my prayers to a benevolent heavenly grandfather, with a long beard ... Somewhat naïve, for sure, but absolutely congruent with corresponding paintings in many churches.*
>
> *As a teenager, I revered the sciences and rejected every concept of a "god". I declared the "Grandfather-God" to be a figure in fairy tales, just as Little Red Riding Hood and Snow White. Without further ado, I left everything behind me, including dolls and teddy bear, and resigned from the church. I felt it inadequate that the church should be understood as background decoration for weddings and that attending a funeral should become so important for people who previ-*

ously hardly ever bothered about religious or spiritual matters.

I took up my search for truth, truthfulness, and the real deep meaning of life.

It was the Indian mystics who gave me the most touching answers.

In their language there were also descriptions of the "Highest" that reminded me of the "Heavenly Father".

But what really interested me was what these mystics embodied, that which became visible and perceptible in their consciousness when I got in spiritual contact with them. The magical acts, some of them surely trumped-up, did not interest them. For them the greatest wonder was when a being could find the way back to its highest essence.

They radiated a grown-up spirituality and they embodied all-embracing love and responsibility for the whole of creation. And, moreover, they taught that we are divine beings.

Worthwhile goals for my journey, I thought. I wanted to learn and grow just here.

In one way or another, at some stage we all deal with God and with death. We try to find definitions and throw them over board later, search anew, walk sinuous paths until we attain, in the best of cases, a mature spirituality.

Finding spirituality is a path.

Some walk this path, although it is often strenuous and confusing, because they do not want to just believe in something based on not knowing.

The following saying, which I heard many years ago, might one day prove true:

"Sooner or later, every seeker becomes a Buddhist. Those who honestly seek will realize at some stage that the

goal is not to follow Buddha, or to worship him. The object is to become Buddha, to become The Enlightened."

In this universe there are only beings. They are all drops of the ocean. Some of them are in contact with their divine potential, some a bit less, and some no longer, because they have distanced themselves from it through actions and happenings.

We are all potentially divine. Therefore, nobody has the right to play god or to rule over us. Those who have such a desire are in the astral levels.

It becomes difficult and extremely narrow, or even fundamental indoctrination, as soon as God is personified and looked upon as a person with a will, who watches over us, punishes us, rewards us or is gracious at his own discretion.

There is no such being in my worldview. I am quite happy to tell you how this image of God dissolved in my case.

The Time when my Personified God Dissolved

It was a significant experience on my journey. I would like to relate it especially for those who do not yet have complete trust in their inherent divine qualities.

After a few years of spiritual exercises and meditation, I fell in a deep hole. It happened unexpectedly. All of a sudden, I was flooded with a feeling of absolute worthlessness. My usual self-esteem and self-confidence were suddenly lost. Instead, I was filled with shame and guilt feelings. What a sorrow and what desperation!

At that time, I sent all my prayers to a "somehow" personified God. But how on Earth could a heavenly being welcome me when I was so worthless?

I did not count the hours I spent weeping. I was in despair. The pivot point of my life was suddenly forever lost. How could my journey continue?

At last a revolutionary spark lit up within me, became more and more powerful and led to the following thoughts:

"If this God, whom I have been talking to so far, is the creator of everything, then he created me as I am now. If I am his product, then he has no other choice but to love me just the way I am!"

Hey! - From that moment onward everything changed. Instead of self-deprecating, I started self-supporting actions and felt up-lifted. I, as a spiritual being, could fully accept myself as a person.

It was such a sweeping change that I was filled with endless love for all of creation. Everything was one. There were no longer any contradictions – and I did no longer need any external entity. Such an entity had just become unthinkable.

Everything is within us. We read this statement over and over again. But when we suddenly really grasp it, it is an unbelievably thrilling moment. At such a moment it becomes true.

Just marginally, but important: When I write about myself, I do not do it because I believe to be someone special. I do it out of respect for your own self-determination. I do not want to influence you, because only you know if a statement is valuable to you or not. In this way, I give maximum scope for your own decisions.

Thought-Out Gods

Convinced that there must be "something greater", many of us create an image of a god. That gives us an address for our prayers. I would like to ask these people whether they know who receives their prayers.

I have seen people treat their God like a friendly neighbour, or like a garden gnome. That does not in the least reflect the maturity of a spiritual dimension. However, it is largely harmless.

The issue becomes dangerous when an astral being comes along and declares himself to be your god. Many of these astral beings are just waiting for such an opportunity. They love to be rendered homage to and to exert influence. Quickly, a few unusual experiences, smaller and bigger miracles are manifested. Nothing is easier for such beings. And again, they have brought one more person under their control. They have played their game for eons. That is how they increase the number of their subordinates.

And this is the way in which thought-out gods come to life. A so far lifeless image suddenly begins to talk, voices are heard. Signals that suggest a power are perceived.

The seeker feels having been heard at last and is overjoyed to receive this long yearned for guidance. He or she does not suspect that the downward spiral towards dependency and bondage has just started turning. How could we ever attain spiritual perfection by simply doing what one is told to do? How could that have anything to do with individual responsibility?

The beings exerting influence are more or less powerful and they all are, without exception, in the astral realm. Some of them strive for more power and want to possess human beings, others express that they mean well. However, since they are themselves unfree, they have a limited perception.

Would they be free beings, they would not seek to influence. Instead, they would just stand by us and serve as orientation.

A further difficulty is that the astral beings cannot be differentiated. Even if they all answer to the same name (e.g. Jesus), they are all astral beings who use a certain mask. They can give themselves whatever appearance they wish.

So, whoever calls or says a prayer, determines himself/herself from which level the answer will come, depending on the consciousness quality and the wishes of the caller. A coarse vibration will attract rough beings, worldly wishes will call for earthbound beings.

Purity, instead, will attract pure beings.

I would like to emphasise again, that all of us on Earth are diligently and meticulously kept away from true spirituality.

A laser-sharp alignment and clear discernment criteria are needed in order to avoid the abyss of astral temptations and to remain free.

Romantic naiveté is hereby quite dangerous!

Highest Spiritual Beings with Divine Qualities

Yes, such beings do exist – thank Heaven.
And they can be contacted.

Many of them never incarnated on Earth as human beings. Others have had several lives and accomplished their journey reaching enlightenment and deliverance.

We all carry the potential to enlightenment and deliverance in us. But only few of us achieve it.

The majority opts for a "better life" instead of striving for spiritual freedom.

Those who have seen enough of this world long for that eternal freedom and bliss.

I have met a few who would not want to reincarnate in this world.

*Does a new incarnation here feel desirable to you?
In that case, you probably did not yet live, experience, enjoy, suffer enough ...
That is perfectly all right.
Take all the time you need.
There is plenty of time available.*

Once deliverance has been attained, the game becomes clear. Freed beings know that every form of interference causes new karma and therefore creates bondage. They will avoid that at all costs.

Freed beings are your best friends when it comes to this inner work. They will never impose themselves on you. Instead they will meet you at eye level, full of love and respect, and be there for you.

They are divine. But they will never act as "gods". They will remind you that you are divine.

They will not solve your problems but with their spiritual succour you can raise your consciousness. That will empower you to find wise solutions to your issues.

My Spiritual Companions

True spiritual companions are of inestimable value in order to avoid blunder. Through my previous incarnations in India, I have a special relationship to some Indian mystics.

Anandamayi Ma is Wonderful

Once I practically knew all books on her by heart, I started contemplating some of the statements and tried to contact her. Her spiritual qualities are to remind me of mine.

Luckily, many pictures of her exist. They helped me to focus my consciousness on hers. She was the first being with whom I could establish a spiritual telepathic contact. A very impressive experience!

I immediately realised that I had been standing in my own way. Master beings - and she is one of them - are much closer to us than we think.

Maharaj Charan Singh

Maharaj Charan Singh is the Master who granted me Initiation.

I strictly followed his teachings during four years. Meditation was easy, the contact was very close, informative and inspiring.

When I discovered that there were no longer any differences between his and my spiritual consciousness, I gave up being his scholar. I did not search for a divine master in order to remain a lifelong scholar …

He is still by my side as a spiritual companion and he is my tuning fork to reassess the quality of my consciousness.

Shri Ramana Maharshi

A source of inspiration for innumerable people.
Very pure, very clear.

Shri Nisargadatta Maharaj

To meet him as being always makes me laugh …

He is full of joy. Wonderful.

Rumi (Dschalal ad-Din ar-Rumi)

He often makes me cry and touches me deeply.

Many other mystics and wise men and women are of great importance to us human beings. The fact that they are not listed here, only means that I have not kept in touch with them.

Spiritual Helpers

We usually call spiritual helpers guardian angels. Many of them protect children. Without this support, many children would not make it to adulthood.

These beings act in accordance with the Higher Self of the children, sometimes also in accordance with the Higher Self of adults. In doing so, they make sure that these people can fulfil their plans. The guardian angels are selfless, they do not take any orders, and they serve in accordance with the spiritual laws.

Heavenly help usually comes unexpectedly and inconspicuously. And still it is quite perceptible for us.

Such helpers cannot avert events resulting from karma, but they most probably can alleviate the consequences.

Getting help when in difficult situations is certainly pleasing. However, in my opinion, we should try to be responsible for ourselves. We have a Higher Self and we can put ourselves at its service.

In our ego-driven society that might sound rather curious. At the time of incarnating on Earth, the majority of us knew that we were free spiritual beings. We have incarnated in order to show and share our light. Definitely not to exploit this planet.

Astral Helpers

I think I have extensively commented on this subject. To work with astral helpers is definitely contrary to spirituality.

The rules are difficult to accept, I know. Whoever pleads for something concerning this world, whether it is prosperity, influence, power, health, or even the ability to heal, will only be heard in the astral realms. There are many beings there willing to help. But they will do it according to their own rules and there is always a price to it.

That is how we become dependent. We ask once, then once more, and then over and over again. Others should get things done for us. We do not want to change anything; we do not want to grow or to develop.

After a while, these beings start playing the role of god in our lives and make sure we understand without any doubt who gives orders.

They will know how to impede our spiritual freedom because we are now their servants.

This has also been described by Goethe in his Dr Faustus. Faust wanted to remain forever young and paid the price with his soul, a price that has eternal consequences. (This subject matter was already well-known before J.W. Goethe. Goethe saw in Dr Faustus his own story. He worked on this subject all of his life.) Whoever feels powerless and longs to do great things can hardly withstand the temptation to form an alliance with the astral beings.

Alliances with magical powers of the astral realms are described in all cultures. Magic has a far greater importance on Earth than I was aware of while writing my first book.

Indigenous people as well as the powerful people on Earth engage in magic. It is mostly visible in the music industry. Elements of magic are used to steer the children and youngsters in the desired direction.

However, we can always set other priorities for ourselves and dissolve situations. It is often those who experienced the danger of astral alliances who clearly chose spirituality as their way.

Dear Reader, Dear Seeker,

It does not matter whether we are trying to forget or if our goal is enlightenment and deliverance. All paths are difficult and painful.

Eternity is long. Very long. It is therefore in any case worthwhile to take pains with the journey and to discover and realise our potential as far as possible, in order to attain a higher perspective.

Understanding a complex issue, or at least taking steps in the right direction, gives us a better feeling than to just draw back and resign: *"Just leave me alone – I cannot take any more!"*

I love to look into the eyes of someone who has just understood a connection, who manages to distance himself/herself from a certain issue, becoming freer and stronger.

And I love to accompany interested persons on their way to their full potential.

But I also know that spiritual knowledge can turn a whole life upside-down. Those who have so far looked at the world from the viewpoint of a victim will find out how it feels to see things from the spiritual point of view. The values are thoroughly jumbled and not seldom even turned around 180 degrees.

I wish all my readers the courage to take this step.

Ruth Huber

Epilogue by Šárka Černochová

The first time Ruth asked me to go back in time up to the point where the mentioned fear had its origin – it was at the main station in Zurich – I thought to myself: "I cannot ever do that."

As a matter of fact, at that time I was completely covered by various emotions blocking my "view". For years I had been feeling sad without any visible reason. Longings for closeness choked me. Meditation remained an empty concept. As soon as I sat down to meditate, I thought of breakfast – that is not funny! – or I fantasised about an embrace. Instead of becoming joyful and free, I became desperate because my search for enlightenment remained fruitless.

At that time, I would not have believed possible that I would one day effortlessly, even on my scooter on the way to work, go back in the timeline to remind beings of their freedom and their wholeness.

The voyage started with "cleaning up" within: coming to terms with my past, my programmes, my dogmas and my vanity; getting over sadness, longings and gridlocked patterns; understanding and liberating foreign entities in my being, until my true self shone through.

I went to working sessions with Ruth Huber. She helped me with what was "up front". I did not have to ruminate my whole childhood, as is commonplace. She placed the emphasis on getting to the heart of things and to work there where understanding and change could take place. In short: true healing.

Ruth is exceptionally precise in her work. Her Higher Self signals when one is just at the right spot. Work is done right there. Everything irrelevant is not looked at.

That makes her work very effective, although not always pleasant. Dissimulations become visible, as well as shameful things and errors that have been committed ... But there is no side-stepping if one wishes to become free or to meditate. Ruth only offers her assistance on the way to truthfulness. Cheating is not possible.

But the voyage and the effort are worthwhile because one becomes increasingly aware of what is supported by the Higher Self and what is not. One's own perception is practiced: On which level am I during meditation? Am I still stuck in the astral realms or is it already a spiritual meditation?

How often did I need Ruth's assistance and supervision until I could distinguish the various "frequencies"! Is my sadness mine or is it the sadness of another being needing help? And, if it is my sadness, when and where did it originate? Did it start recently or hundreds of thousands of years ago? And, was I incarnated at that time or was I without a body? Are sparks of consciousness of other beings stuck on me, which need to be liberated so that I am myself again? Where did they come from? Or perhaps my Body Intelligence has a problem?

These are all important questions in order to find which tools are necessary for understanding and clearing up the issues at hand, thereby becoming freer and lighter.

Ruth's work requires great knowledge, which she shares. It is not only inspiring but unbelievably useful. Arachnophobia, headaches, anger, lack of energy can have various causes. Each problem has to be looked at individually. In other words: even small issues offer learning possibilities and one becomes richer.

Once everything stressful had disappeared through truthful work, I finally found myself effortlessly in the "up-wind", meditation. With all of the many rough and stirred up feelings and all the contradictions in me, I could not have possibly passed through the eye of the needle into spirituality. Additionally, many astral beings had taken possession of my mind. My thoughts quietened down once I had liberated the astral beings – at the beginning with Ruth's help, later by myself. It felt as though everything separating me from peace and love had just fallen off.

The Chart you will find in this book also helped me to meditate. The chakras and the levels are important orientation points. At the beginning, in the learning phase, one can just climb the ladder, step-by-step up to Heaven.

I went through a very difficult phase the moment I decided I was ready to "leave the prison". I don't mean temporarily, in meditation. That was already possible at an earlier stage. What I mean is to leave the prison and be aligned with the Source in my whole way of being, my attitude; not being under the influence of the prison guards. The step into freedom. To have the certainty to be able to choose freely where I would want to go after death, not having to reincarnate if I do not wish to do so.

The astral powers did not want to lose me and placed many obstacles wherever possible. For example, I became very tired every time I wanted to do spiritual work, and so I was prevented from doing it. I was just too tired to recognise the beings behind the obstacles. During a working session with Ruth, I managed to liberate myself from their influence, finding my own power to continue my work, taking the next steps.

Nobody can imagine how much support and solidarity Ruth offers to her students while they stand at this threshold, thereby being herself massively attacked. I do not believe that this crossing can be walked by on one's own.

I would not stand here where I stand today without the working sessions with Ruth Huber. I would never have been able to develop the effective methods nor to acquire the necessary awareness on my own.

To work with Ruth is the most important decision I took in my life. I am very thankful to have met her.

Hoping that many already capable human beings wish to become even more capable and free – our planet needs such people urgently – I am pleased to see all the ones who make good use of the time while Ruth is still here in her human body.

I wish you an enlightening voyage!

Šárka Černochová   January 30, 2013

scharka@cernochova.ch

Ruth Huber

The author was born in Zurich in 1950. She opened her practice for body work in 1983. As researching consciousness and finding answers to questions such as "Who are we? Where do we come from? What is death?" became fundamental for Ruth Huber, she meditated her way in the greatest and most important adventure of her life: she learned the relationship between the various levels of consciousness, the existence of the Higher Self, i.e. she re-discovered those qualities.

Having found fulfilment in this knowledge and in view of the many seekers, she began accompanying people in their consciousness opening process.

In 2002 Ruth Huber presented a detailed and easily understood description of the astral and spiritual realms in her book *"Remembering. Those who remember gain consciousness"*

The knowledge shared in the book is based on her own research, her experiences, as well as the experiences of friends, clients, deceased persons, and on telepathic work with spiritual beings.

In 2012 she published *"Stranded Angels. A handbook for all those who find life on Earth rather confusing."* In this book Ruth Huber explains the rules of the game here on Earth to the newcomers.

For Ruth Huber it is inerasably clear that we all come from divine consciousness – and that we are capable of contacting this enlightened essence. We all carry the potential to perfection within. It is helpful to have someone like Ruth Huber standing by our side. Someone who has personally gone through all the challenges of the path.

We all have existed long before we incarnated here on Earth. We have more or less identified ourselves with being human beings, not only forgetting our spiritual origins but also our connection to all the beings out there in the endless universe.

Realizing our potential and again experiencing ourselves as spiritual beings, will enable us to communicate with our star brothers and sisters. Some of them have been waiting for long for our awakening.

www.ruth-huber.ch

Too much energy	Too little energy	Chakra
If the 6th chakra is un-enlightened and disconnected, only the intellect works (the intellect is a sub-function of consciousness). Concepts and theories are read, compared, repeated without being able to experience truthfulness by means of feelings, emotions and life experience.		6th Chakra
Talks incessantly. Likes to be in the limelight. Fake humour (repeats old successful jokes). Playful.	Does not find the correct words. Falls silent to avoid being called arrogant. Incapable of developing solutions or implementing them. Opportunist.	5th Chakra
Gives and gives and gives … Wants to help everybody. Always moved to tears. Never ending longing …	Always striving to be loved. Having friends increases self-worth.	4th Chakra
Excessive aggression, ruthlessness. POWER - powerless	Cannot fill its own space. Poor self-worth. Subordinates. POWERLESS - power	3rd Chakra
Very sensual, possibly over-sexualised.	Needy, affectionate, tearful, needs confirmation from others. Attunes to the exterior emotional mood.	2nd Chakra
Greed, hoarding, material safeguarding, material thinking.	Fear of life, feels constantly endangered, existential fear, panic.	1st Chakra

Getting stuck	Chakra is enlightened
Disconnected from life and love. Often the case with scientists. Research disconnected from life.	Enlightenment is only possible if the other chakras are redeemed and connected.
Ego, vanity: "Nothing works if I don't take care of it myself." Intolerance, Arrogance. If without love: cynical, sarcastic.	Sees, recognises, <u>understands</u>. If needed, can be adequately creative, visionary, playful, precise.
Cannot take decisions. Feelings dictate behaviour. Believes that he/she should love everybody. Constant sympathy.	Radiant, warm and compassionate. The heart is invulnerable.
Winning and losing. Always needs a culprit. Wants to be brilliant, to prove things ...	Healthy, adequate self-worth, relaxed force.
Remains needy and delegates responsibility. Feels as one half of the relationship. The eternal victim. Self-pity.	Integrated sensuality, joy of living.
Remaining stuck in existential issues. Health becomes an end in itself. Anxiety.	Primal sense of trust.

Those Who Remember Gain Consciousness

Long before we had a body, even long before there were bodies, there was consciousness, there existed spiritual beings. We all come from the numinous source and are filled by the desire for truth and love we can reconnect.

An impressive Model helps to clearly structure this path of truth and love.

Stranded Angels.
A Handbook tor all those who find life on Earth rather confusing

Looking at planet Earth from a spiritual point of view, one will see numerous beings who have distanced themselves from their potential, beings who have stranded.

It is really helpful to be able to discern what belongs to "Heaven", i.e. to the spiritual spheres, what belongs in the illusionary astral realms, and which rules apply here on Earth.

www.ruth-huber.ch

www.ingramcontent.com/pod-product-compliance
Lightning Source LLC
Chambersburg PA
CBHW071152160426
43196CB00011B/2057